BCS BREAKTHROUGH

UTAH'S HISTORIC 2004 SEASON

BY DIRK FACER

PRODUCTION CREDITS

ISBN: 0-9758769-1-0
ISBN: Limited Edition Leatherbound 0-9758769-2-9

Published By:
KCI Sports Ventures, LLC
1402 Quail Run Drive
Savoy, IL 61874

Editor: Peter J. Clark
Photo Editor: Tom Smart
Dustjacket Design: Terry Neutz Hayden
Booklayout and Design: Terry Neutz Hayden

Photos Courtesy of *Deseret Morning News*. Photos for Arizona game courtesy of *Arizona Daily Star* and photographers Jim Davis and Jeffry Scott.

Printed and bound by Worzalla Publishing, Stevens Point, WI.

TOM SMART

A Special Thanks to *Deseret Morning News* Photography Department

It is a pure pleasure to photo edit this book commemorating University of Utah's historic football season. Having photographed Utah sporting events for over 25 years, both for the *Deseret Morning News* and the University of Utah Athletic Department, nothing quite compares to this season. The *Deseret Morning News* photo department made a commitment to follow the Utes to all their games (with the exception of Arizona because of the late deadline), and as a result have been able to produce an amazing photographic documentation of this season. Truly, this is perhaps the best photojournalistic record of any athletic season in Utah's history. There are several reasons for this, the most important being content (it was simply an amazing year), but technology was also a huge factor. With the new digital age of photography, the quality is actually better than film–especially in low lighting. The speed of transmission and editing enabled photographers to shoot more of the game and still make newspaper deadlines. In the past, shooting night football was a distinct disadvantage, however, with the new lighting installed for the Olympics and the new field, which reflects more light, the quality of the photos is unparalleled. Unless credited otherwise, seven staff photographers and Mitch Dumke, an 18-year-old student freelancer for the paper shot all the photos for this book. Special thanks go to Chuck Wing for his excellent help in editing much of the BYU game and the Fiesta Bowl. To have photos displayed in such a lasting, high quality format, rather than the bottom of the birdcage after two days, is a treat any newspaper photographer relishes. I hope the Utah fans will enjoy this as much as we do.

Tom Smart
Photo Editor

JEFFREY D. ALLRED

MICHAEL BRANDY

RAVELL CALL

MITCHELL THOMAS DUMKE

AUGUST MILLER

TOM SMART

SCOTT G. WINTERTON

CHUCK WING

ACKNOWLEDGEMENT

The publisher would like to offer a "very special thank you" to the following for their efforts and contributions to this book:

Head Coach Urban Meyer, his staff and all of the Utah players–without your outstanding efforts there wouldn't be a book. Dr. Chris Hill and the University of Utah athletic department for their assistance and support of this book. Special thanks to Pete Oliszczak, Liz Abel, and Doug Archie. Terry Neutz-Hayden for sharing your talented design abilities, your continued friendship and always cheerful demeanor. Tom Smart for your tireless effort in accumulating and editing the fantastic photos found in this book. The many talented photographers who contributed photos to this project. Dirk Facer, Mike Sorenson and Linda Hamilton for recapturing an unforgettable season. Bret Kroencke for your behind the scenes work.

Sheila Jasenovsky, Kim Deuel, Tony Gindt and the dynamite staff at Worzalla Publishing for their hard work in getting this book printed on time. Doug Milkowski, Jason "Bird" Beherendt, Bob Raczek . . . Tonia Hanutke, Shawn Herzog and Alex Gibson . . . Leif Eckholm, Bob Nelson, Jerry Fitzgerald and all the others I may be overlooking, but whose efforts are certainly much appreciated.

Peter Clark
Publisher

JEFFREY D. ALLRED

BCS BREAKTHROUGH

CONTENT

MICHAEL BRADY

MESSAGE FROM COACH MEYER

2004 was a very special year for the University of Utah and the Salt Lake City community. The unprecedented national exposure reflected the greatness of the University students, faculty, and fans. There was no greater feeling than walking out of the tunnel at Rice-Eccles Stadium and seeing the enthusiastic support of "The MUSS" and then at the end of the game seeing all those same students waiting to celebrate with its team. I salute you all for that, you gave the Utes home field advantage in every game we played, both home and away.

None of this would have even been possible without the 105 players that lined up day-in and day-out the whole year. January 12, 2004 you started out working harder than every team in the country. You invested more time, energy, and your soul into a common goal, to be the best college football team in the country, and you did it. There will be nothing that anyone can do to take away what you accomplished this year, PERFECTION! Individually we all ran into obstacles both on and off the field, however, as a team we were perfect and that is something no one else can claim. I thank you for everything you have done for this team. I can not express the appreciation that I have for each and every one of you, and I will forever remember this season and this team.

-Urban Meyer

Coach Urban Meyer

AUGUST MILLER

FOREWORD

It couldn't have worked out better if I had planned it.

After 38 years of broadcasting Utah football, I thought I'd seen just about everything. Nine coaches hired and all but one fired. Ray Nagel left to go to Iowa. A couple of 1-10 seasons and a couple of 10-2 seasons. In 2003, Urban Meyer's inaugural season ended with a 10-2 mark and Utah's first outright conference championship in 46 years. The 2004 season looked promising. Heading into my final year as the "Voice of the Utes," I sensed the anticipation.

BEN CROSBY

Bill Marcroft, being honored by Utah Athletic Director Chris Hill, at halftime of the BYU game, his last home game of doing play by play.

The Utes' theme for 2004 was "You ain't seen nothing yet!" Equally optimistic about a team that had almost everybody back, I began every game by calling Utah a "team of destiny." Coach Meyer took exception with the expression though, saying it implied his team would win no matter how hard they prepared. However, it was obvious to me this team was special and their "fate" an unforgettable place in college football history.

Utah had the best staff of coaches ever assembled as well as players with a unique combination of athleticism and intelligence. Four starters had already graduated, a first for a Utah team. Quarterback Alex Smith, just a junior, was working on his master's degree in economics. Academic All-American free safety Morgan Scalley was in graduate school, along with running back Marty Johnson and center Jesse Boone. Utah also had a perfect schedule, set to play teams from the Big 12, ACC, and Pac 10–all Bowl Championship Series (BCS) conferences–allowing the Utes to showcase their abilities against top-flight competition. This would be the season to bring Utah into the elite of college football and the BCS.

Utah began the season ranked #21 in the nation. The Utes beat Texas A&M 31-21 in the season opener. When Arizona fell 23-6 and then North Carolina 46-16, and having beaten Utah State, Air Force, and New Mexico along the way, Utah was in the top ten and the BCS poll for the first time in its football history. Everybody started to believe in the team's destiny. The campus bookstore made a record profit on the sale of Utah memorabilia, so much so that it was able to reduce the price of textbooks to Utah students for the rest of the year. Sellouts and record attendance were the norm. The Utes rose as high as fifth in the polls, and when they beat rival BYU 52-21 in the final game of the season, the field at Rice-Eccles Stadium disappeared in a sea of red.

The 2004 Utes fulfilled their destiny–an undefeated season and a bid to the Fiesta Bowl. They will be known as the first mid-major conference team to break into the BCS. Alex Smith was named *The Sporting News and Sport Illustrated* College Football Player of the Year and a Heisman Trophy finalist. Smith, along with Morgan Scalley and offensive tackle Chris Kemoeatu, was named to the second team of the Associated Press All-American squad. Scalley also became Utah's first two-time Academic All-American. Coach Urban Meyer was named National Coach of the Year.

As "fate" would have it, I was able to end my career as the "Voice of the Utes" with the greatest season in the 112-year history of Utah football.

Truly a team of destiny.

Bill Marcroft

UTAH
UTAH

MICHAEL BRADY

TOM SMART

SCOTT G. WINTERTON

TOM SMART

INTRODUCTION TRAINING CAMP

Setting the Tone for a Championship

On the eve of training camp, Utah coach Urban Meyer conducted a long team meeting. "We discussed expectations," he said. "Not polls and those kind of things. Just expectations on the practice field, which is all that matters." After going 10-2 and winning their first outright conference title since 1957, the Utes were eager to get back on the field. A fitting encore, though, would be pursued only in segments. Meyer insisted the only three measurable ways to evaluate the program involved performance, attitude and behavior. And so, on a warm August day in Salt Lake City, high expectations for 2004 began to be tackled.

Following the NCAA-mandated five-day acclimation period, the Utes began in earnest what proved to be their finest season – an 11-0 record and a historic berth in the Bowl Championship Series. First things first, though. "This summer was crazy. Last summer, we were kind of like 'Man, we're getting worked so hard. Man, I can't believe we are working this hard. Why are they working us this hard? I've never been worked like this,' " said senior linebacker Corey Dodds. "This summer we're working harder and we're kind of like 'Are we working hard enough? Do you think we're going to be as good as we're supposed to be? Are we working as hard as we need to, to be as good as we want to be?' "Those kind of questions I get from people," Doods continued. "That just shows the character. They want to be the best." The comments made Meyer smile. "It comes down to attitude, chemistry and a senior walking off (the practice field) telling you that they want to work harder," Meyer said. "I'm glad Corey Dodds said that. It just made my day."

Before practice each day, Meyer has the Utes run a dozen 20-yard dashes at full speed. It's proven to be quite a gauge for the program he and his staff are building. Unlike 2003, he noted, there was no moaning or complaining. "That is a great sign," Meyer said. "That's the sign of a team that has focused. They're not worried about how many periods we are going in practice. I haven't heard that one time. Last year, it seemed like people would say, 'Why are we doing this?' Now they know why we're doing it." It's an evolution, of sorts – played out daily on an intense level. Dodds said there's no time to rest on past laurels. "Everyone has got to come out and think we have to learn," Dodds said. "We have to learn, and we have to be better every single day. Every day; it doesn't matter if you're a vet. So what if you played last year? Say you played three seasons, this is your senior year and you've been a starter since you were a freshman. So what? This is a new year, and you've got to get better." Continual improvement is a major component in Meyer's philosophy. Idleness isn't tolerated, even by those sidelined with injuries. Meyer, thus, created "The Pit." Instead of having injured players sit under a tent drinking water during practice, as he observed as a player at Cincinnati and as an assistant coach at Notre Dame, he found a way to make every trainer, manager, coach and player leave the practice field with a feeling of accomplishment. "Players don't look at it as punishment," said Meyer. "That's their work." Those sidelined with minor injuries and ailments spend practice in a marked-off area. Police tape is the current marker of choice. They do a variety of exercises under the watchful eye of trainers. Stationary bikes and weights are used, as are nontraditional items such as heavy chains and rocks. "We got a saying," said Meyer. "Take care of The Pit or The Pit takes care of you." Translation: There's no such thing as time off. Meyer began the practice at Bowling Green and has continued it at Utah. "I was not a good player (in college)," Meyer said, "but I played the game and would get sick to my stomach when I would walk off the field and the guys that didn't practice, they're sitting there eating food and I can barely lift my arms. So I always felt like – and it's human nature – I hated those people who didn't practice." Seeing as many as 25 players sitting around a tent drinking water at Notre Dame reenforced his feelings. He vowed as a head coach it wouldn't happen. And as players at Bowling Green and Utah can attest, it hasn't. "Kids hate to get in that sucker," said defensive line coach Gary Andersen. "You get yourself in The Pit and you're going to work your fanny off until you're able to get back on the practice field."

Utah players stretch out during training camp at Ute Field in August.

SCOTT G. WINTERTON

Time, Meyer believes, is a precious commodity. Opportunities come and go with indecisiveness. "He's like a lot of guys I was with early," said cornerbacks coach Chuck Heater, "both as a player and as a coach, guys that cross the T's and dot the I's. Everybody has accountability and nothing really goes unnoticed. He's a guy that's really thorough and on top of things." Everything is planned down to the minute, noted Andersen. Check that, it's planned down to the second. "You know exactly what direction you're going and exactly what's expected to keep the kids at a high pace," he said. It's the only speed Meyer can appreciate. "The kids compete daily and the way they're pushed to be able to have to win or lose every single day, I think, is a very important factor," Andersen said. "It really helps the football team." And that, after all, is what Meyer was hired to do.

40

TOM SMART

Opposite: *Ute defenders deliver a bone-jarring hit early on against Texas A&M.*

Right: *Wide receiver Steve Savoy, left, celebrates after scoring one of his two touchdowns in Utah's season-opening win over Texas A&M.*

GAME 1: Utah 41, Texas A&M 21

Thursday, September 2, 2004: Salt Lake City

	AP TOP 25	ESPN/USA TODAY	BCS
Preseason	20	21	n/a
SEPTEMBER 5	17	16	n/a

SCOTT G. WINTERTON

Alex Smith throws three touchdown passes and runs for two more scores as the Utes open the season with a victory over a Big 12 Conference team on ESPN.

So far, so good for the 19th-ranked Utes.

Alex Smith threw for 359 yards and three touchdowns and ran for two more scores as Utah opened the season with a 41-21 victory over Texas A&M at Rice-Eccles Stadium.

The game was played before a capacity crowd of 45,419 and a national television audience on ESPN.

"We just beat Texas A&M and that doesn't happen often at a school like Utah. A Mountain West team isn't supposed to beat a top-shelf Big 12 team," said Utah coach Urban Meyer. "So I'm very proud of our effort."

Running back Marty Johnson ran for a team-high 77 yards in his first game in nearly two years. He was pleased with how the Utes performed on both sides of the ball.

Top Right: *Utah running back Marty Johnson eludes a Texas A&M defender. He finished with a team-high 77 yards rushing in his first game in nearly two years.*

Bottom Right: *Members of "The MUSS," Utah's student fan club, display their team spirit before a packed house and a national television audience on ESPN.*

Below: *Utah quarterback Alex Smith unloads a pass. The junior connected with wide receiver Steve Savoy on a 78-yard scoring strike just over a minute into the opener against Texas A&M.*

AUGUST MILLER

TOM SMART

SCOTT G. MILLER

"On defense, if we can keep doing this we'll be tough to beat," he said. "And it's great to play with a quarterback like Alex. They can't really key on the run. They have to respect both games."

Smith set the pace offensively by completing 21-of-29 passes. Paris Warren led the Utes with seven catches.

"We played a good team on the road tonight," said Texas A&M coach Dennis Franchione. "Alex Smith had a great game, and if he continues to play as well as he did tonight, Utah will be tough to beat."

Meyer's concern about weathering a first-half storm proved to be unfounded. Unlike last season's 28-26 loss in College Station, when Texas A&M jumped out to a 21-0 halftime lead, the Utes came out strong both offensively and defensively.

They held a 27-7 advantage at the break despite losing four contributors to injury - two, however, returned in the second half.

"I thought this would be the hardest 10 minutes we had ever gone through together," said Meyer.

Utah scored on its third play from scrimmage when quarterback Alex Smith teamed with wide receiver Steve Savoy on a 78-yard touchdown pass. The longest scoring play in the Meyer era capped a game-opening drive that took just 1:13 off the clock.

Early in the second quarter, after Utah's defense extended its streak to 11 shutout quarters over four games dating back to last November, the Utes doubled their lead.

One play after a 24-yard run by Smith, Savoy ran nine yards for a touchdown to make it 14-0.

It stayed that way for more than 7 1/2 minutes. That's when Utah reached the end zone for the third time. A sustained drive that covered 65 yards on seven plays, including a 45-yard pass to Travis LaTendresse, was concluded by a 7-yard TD run by Smith.

After forcing Texas A&M to punt for the sixth consecutive series, the Utes marched downfield again. A 38-yard touchdown pass from Smith to John Madsen increased the lead to 27-0 (kicker Bryan Borreson's PAT attempt hit the left goal post and missed) with 3:52 to play in the half.

The Aggies responded this time around and became the first team since Wyoming last November to score on Utah's defense. The shutout streak lasted 292 days and spanned games against the Cowboys, BYU and Southern Mississippi. It came to an end with 3:02 remaining in the second quarter when Texas A&M quarterback Reggie McNeal scrambled 59 yards for a touchdown on a third-and 4 situation.

The play increased the Aggies' total offense to 140 yards. They managed just 81 over their first 28 plays - much of which came against a depleted Utah defense. Safeties Eric Weddle and Kawika Casco, as well as nose guard

Junior college transfer Fano Tagovailoa and his teammates had plenty of reason to celebrate in Utah's decisive victory over Texas A&M. The Utes avenged last season's loss in College Station with an impressive performance.

MITCH DUMKE

Steve Fifita, left the game with knee injuries early in the game.

Weddle (MCL tear in his left leg) and Casco (blown right knee) wound up watching the rest of the game on crutches. Fifita, however, returned to play in the third quarter-as did Savoy, who had an X-ray taken of his ribs just before halftime.

Despite the lopsided score, Meyer said the Utes had some major issues to overcome.

Utah regained its momentum following the intermission when Smith finished a six-play drive with a 37-yard touchdown run.

The defense also got rejuvenated.

Linebackers Corey Dodds and Tommy Hackenbruck stopped Texas A&M running back Courtney Lewis at the goal line on fourth down just before the third quarter came to a close.

And though Utah's new shutout streak proved to be shortlived – the Aggies scored on short runs by McNeal and Jason Carter down the stretch – it failed to tarnish a stellar effort.

"We deserved this one. We worked so hard," said Scalley. "People go down and people step up. This game says a lot about our character."

Between the A&M scores, Smith teamed with Jerome Wright on a 13-yard touchdown pass to keep the game well out of reach.

"I'm glad we're done with them," Meyer said of the two-year series with the Aggies. "I don't want to see A&M again for a long time because I know what they're going to look like in the next year or two.

Right: *Defensive end Jonathan Fanene and the rest of Utah's defense held Texas A&M's offense to just seven points through three quarters of play.*

PAGE 15
Top Left: *Utah linebacker Corey Dodds led the Utes with two tackles-for-loss in the victory over Texas A&M.*
Top Right: *Quarterback Alex Smith steps into the end zone for one of his two rushing touchdowns. He guided the Utes to victory with three passes and two rushes for scores.*
Bottom: *Freshman cornerback Ryan Smith is congratulated by teammate Fano Tanovailoa after recording his first collegiate interception.*

TOM SMART

GAME 1 RECAP

Aggies	0	7	0	14	– 21
UTES	7	20	7	7	– 41

UTAH – Steve Savoy 78 pass from Alex Smith (Bryan Borreson kick) 13:47, 1st
UTAH – Savoy 9 run (Borreson kick) 14:53, 2nd
UTAH – Smith 7 run (Borreson kick) 7:20, 2nd
UTAH – John Madsen 38 pass from Smith (Borreson kick failed) 3:52, 2nd
A&M – McNeal 59 run (Pegram kick) 3:02, 2nd
UTAH – Smith 37 run (Borreson kick) 8:58, 3rd
A&M – McNeal 8 run (Pegram kick) 11:35, 4th
UTAH – Jerome Wright 13 pass from Smith (Borreson kick) 7:00, 4th
A&M – Carter 5 run (Pegram kick) 0:10, 4th

Texas A&M	Final Statistics	UTAH
17	First Downs	23
167	Net Rushing	212
270	Passing Yards	370
74-437	Total Offense	76-582
26:56	Time of Possession	33:04

TOM SMART

SCOTT G. WINTERTON

Opposite: Utah wide reciever Steve Savoy catches a TD pass in the first quarter out leaping Arizona's Antonie Cason for the first score of the game.

Right: Steve Savoy, who scored two of Utah's three touchdowns in Arizona, is brought down by Lamon Means of the Wildcats.

GAME 2: Utah 23, Arizona 6

Saturday, September 11, 2004: Tucson, Ariz.

	AP TOP 25	ESPN/USA TODAY	BCS
SEPTEMBER 12	15	14	N/A

Photos courtesy of Arizona Daily Star
BY JEFFRY SCOTT

Utes prevail in Pac-10 country by recovering three fumbles and intercepting a pass. The offense does its part by scoring on its first three possessions.

TUCSON, Ariz. - Utah handled the heat at Arizona Stadium.

On a warm and sticky night in the desert, the 17th-ranked Utes claimed a 23-6 victory over Arizona. They forced a turnover while scoring on their first three possessions to lay the foundation for their second win.

The successful start proved necessary as penalties took a toll (eight for 82 yards in the game) and Arizona's loud crowd of 52,790 (largest since the final game of 2000) helped make things more difficult. It wasn't enough, however, to prevent the Utes from winning their sixth straight game, a streak dating back to last season's triple overtime victory at Air Force.

"Our defense really stepped it up in the second half," said Utah coach Urban Meyer. "The best thing about this game is we did not play our best and we just beat a Pac-10 team and beat them on their home turf."

Photos courtesy of Arizona Daily Star
BY JIM DAVIS

Photos courtesy of Arizona Daily Star and photographers Jim Davis and Jeffry Scott

Left: *Utah defensive back Antonio Young makes a tackle during the road victory at Arizona.*

Bottom Right: *Utah's Steve Savoy breaks away from Arizona's Antoine Cason after one of his seven catches. Savoy had 95 yards and two touchdowns.*

GAME 2 RECAP

UTES	17	0	6	0	– 23
Wildcats	3	3	0	0	– 6

UTAH – Bryan Borreson 21 FG, 12:07, 1st
UTAH – Steve Savoy 5 pass from Alex Smith (Borreson kick) 6:21, 1st
ARIZONA – Folk 33 FG, 2:10, 1st
UTAH – Marty Johnson 20 run (Borreson kick) 1:17, 1st
ARIZONA – Folk 35 FG, 10:23, 2nd
UTAH – Savoy 9 pass from Smith (Borreson kick failed) 1:07, 3rd
ARIZONA – Carter 5 run (Pegram kick) 0:10, 4th

UTAH	Final Statistics	Arizona
18	First Downs	18
38-156	Net Rushing	33-114
170	Passing Yards	198
326	Total Offense	312
28:24	Time of Possession	31:36

Photos courtesy of Arizona Daily Star BY JIM DAVIS

By game's end, Utah's defense had recovered three fumbles and an interception to offset 312 yards of total offense by the Wildcats-just 14 fewer than the Ute tally.

"I guess it was just bend but don't break. We gave up too many yards but four take-aways makes up for that," said safety Morgan Scalley. "We have a lot that we need to work on. We know our defense is better than that. Our main goal is to win. We win, then we can work on the rest."

The defense got things started by causing Arizona tailback Mike Bell to fumble on the game's first play from scrimmage. Middle linebacker Tommy Hackenbruck jarred the ball loose when he hit Bell and Scalley recovered it for the Utes on the Wildcat 23.

Six plays later, Bryan Borreson's 21-yard field goal made it 3-0. After forcing Arizona to punt on the ensuing possession, Utah added a touchdown to its lead.

A 5-yard scoring strike from Alex Smith to Steve Savoy gave the Utes some breathing room with 6:21 left to play in the quarter.

Trailing 10-0, Arizona responded by making its first field goal since September 27, 2003. Nick Folk capped a 10-play drive with a 33-yard kick to put the Wildcats on the board.

Utah needed less than a minute to retaliate.

After moving into scoring position on a 38-yard pass from Smith to Paris Warren and a 14-yard run by Quinton Ganther, the Utes extended their advantage to 17-3. Marty Johnson's first touchdown in nearly two years came on a 20-yard run up the middle. The late first-quarter TD ended Utah's scoring for the half.

Arizona cut into the deficit with a 35-yard field goal by Folk early in the second quarter, but failed to convert on an opportunity to add more points just before the intermission.

The Wildcats had three chances to score from the Utah 1-yard line in the final two minutes. Hackenbruck stopped running back Chris Henry at the line of scrimmage on the first attempt before nose guard Steve Fifita found similar success against fullback Gilbert Harris on the next play.

The goal-line stand concluded with Casey Evans forcing Harris to fumble on fourth down. Hackenbruck scooped it up on the Utah 2 to end the threat. The Utes then simply ran out the remaining 49 seconds of the half and led 17-6 at the break-despite running 10 fewer plays and an 8 1/2-minute disadvantage on time of possession.

Fortunately for Utah, its defense made up the difference. The Utes made two big plays in the third quarter while the offense sputtered under the weight of penalties.

The first, an interception by defensive tackle Sione Pouha deep in Arizona territory, set up a 9-yard touchdown throw from Smith to Savoy. Borreson's PAT attempt hit the right post and fell to the ground, leaving the score 23-6.

An unsportsmanlike penalty-Savoy was flagged for spinning the ball in celebration after the score-and a kick out of bounds led to Arizona beginning its next series at midfield. The Wildcats managed to drive inside the Utah 10 before Spencer Toone, who recorded a game-high 13 tackles, recovered a fumble by Bell to end the threat.

The fourth quarter featured several punt exchanges and a missed field goal by Arizona as the Utes managed to protect their lead down the stretch.

Smith, who improved to 11-1 as Utah's starter, completed 12-of-22 passes for 170 yards to lead the offense. Savoy finished with a game-high seven receptions, while Johnson had 105 yards rushing.

Utah wide rreceiver Steve Savoy makes one of his seven catches against the Wildcats.

Photos courtesy of Arizona Daily Star and photographers Jim Davis and Jeffry Scott

UTAH
UTAH
29
93

Opposite: A group of Utah defenders celebrate after cornerback Ryan Smith recovers a fumble in the lopsided win at Utah State.

Right: Alex Smith completed nine passes for 163 yards and a touchdown in limited action at Utah State. He also rushed for 44 yards and a score before giving way to back-ups Brian Johnson and Fano Tagovailoa after the Utes built a 41-0 halftime lead.

GAME 3: Utah 48, Utah State 6

Saturday, September 18, 2004: Logan, Utah

	AP TOP 25	ESPN/USA TODAY	BCS
SEPTEMBER 19	14	14	n/a

TOM SMART

Visiting Utes jump out to a 41-0 halftime lead to prevail in the annual "Battle of the Brothers." Biggest margin of victory over Utah State since 1950.

LOGAN - So much for "Battle of the Brothers." The 104th meeting between Utah and Utah State wasn't much of a fight. Or a football game, for that matter.

The 15th-ranked Utes extended their winning streak over the Aggies to seven games with a 48-6 victory.

They led 41-0 at halftime en route to their largest margin of victory in the series since a 46-0 win in 1950. Utah's point total was its highest ever against USU.

"The thing that was most impressive is this is three games in a row that we came out smoking in the first quarter," said Utah coach Urban Meyer. "And I think that's preparation and guys excited about playing this game."

USU fans caught an early break when the Romney Stadium scoreboard malfunctioned. It was turned off for

TOM SMART

Top Right: *Defensive end Jonathan Fanene rambled 76 yards for a touchdown after intercepting a Utah State pass late in the second quarter.*

Bottom Right: *Utah fans of all shapes, sizes and headwear made the trip to Logan to support the Utes in the annual "Battle of the Brothers."*

Below: *Utah center Jesse Boone anchors the offensive line.*

TOM SMART

TOM SMART

SCOTT G. WINTERTON

much of the first quarter while Utah built a 20-0 advantage.

Short touchdown runs by Paris Warren (four yards), Marty Johnson (one yard) and Alex Smith (seven yards) capped scoring drives during the decisive stretch, while the defense held USU to minus-5 yards.

"I really liked the first quarter, especially our defense to keep them pinned down in there. We'll take the win. It went perfectly as scripted," said Meyer. "I think when we play defense as we play, a lot of offenses can score when you get in a short field like we got today."

The Aggies failed to get a single first down until the final play of the first quarter. It came on a promising series that eventually led to the Utah 1-yard line. The Utes, however, wound up making their third goal-line stand in three weeks. A fourth-down interception by linebacker Corey Dodds put an end to the threat and ushered in another successful offensive series for Utah.

"That was a huge play in the red zone," said linebacker Spencer Toone, who finished with six tackles-sharing team-high honors with Kyle Brady. "We came up big."

Six plays and just over two minutes later, Quinton Ganther's 2-yard run extended the Utes' lead to 27-0 midway through the second quarter. Before the half was complete, two more touchdowns would be added to the tally.

After forcing USU to punt for the fourth time, Utah embarked upon its longest drive of the season - a 92-yard march that ended with a 10-yard scoring strike from Smith to Warren.

Trailing 34-0, USU responded by moving downfield into the red zone for the second time. And just like the first trip, the Aggies saw their work quickly unfold when quarterback Travis Cox threw an interception. Defensive tackle Siona Pouha deflected the pass and Jonathan Fanene caught it. The defensive end returned it 76 yards for a touchdown to put an exclamation point on Utah's dominating first-half performance.

"I wasn't worrying about somebody tackling me," said the 6-foot-3, 290-pound senior. "I just wanted to take it to the house."

At the break, the Utes had 301 yards of offense and were a perfect 5-for-5 inside the red zone. The Aggies, meanwhile, managed just 104 yards and converted on only 1-of-9 third-down opportunities.

"We came out and were able to do the things we planned on," said Toone. "We had a good scheme and we were able to execute it."

In the second half, as the announced crowd of 24,750 began to dwindle and mass substitutions were made, Utah's season-long streak of avoiding a turnover came to an end when back-up quarterback Brian Johnson was intercepted-on a deflected pass-by USU cornerback Jarrett Bush early in the third quarter. The Aggies capitalized on the

Tight end Blake Burdette heads downfield after making a catch in Utah's 48-6 win at Utah State.

TOM SMART

brief momentum shift to score their only points in the game. Working with a short field, they moved 55 yards on seven plays for a touchdown. The score came on an 8-yard pass from Cox to Tarrell Richards.

Utah retaliated on its next possession after Derrek Richards returned the kickoff 40 yards. Johnson, a 17-year-old freshman, redeemed his earlier miscue by connecting with John Madsen for his first career TD pass – an 8-yarder with 3:50 to go in the third quarter. It closed the door on the Utes' highest scoring game since racking up 52 points against South Florida on October 6, 2001.

"I think they executed their offense pretty well. Defensively they were really strong. The thing that really hurt us in the first half was field position," said USU coach Mick Dennehy. "We just didn't have the ability early in the game . . . I think Utah is every bit as good as their ranking."

Defensive coordinator Kyle Whittingham credited the Utes for setting the tone by dominating the line of scrimmage from the first snap. Contributions were plentiful as 32 players made tackles.

Offensively, Marty Johnson led all rushers with 76 yards on 11 carries in his first start of 2004. Smith played just half the game, but completed 9-of-12 passes for 163 yards and a touchdown.

For USU, Cox was 17-of-28 for 163 yards with two interceptions and a touchdown. Kevin Robinson finished with a game-high seven receptions.

Right: *Utah running back Marty Johnson celebrates after scoring a touchdown on a 1-yard run in the first quarter at Utah State.*

PAGE 25
Top left: *Tailback Marty Johnson slips past a Utah State defender while picking up a chunk of his game-high 76 yards rushing.*

Top right: *Utah cheerleaders run down the sideline with a "U" flag after one of many Ute scores in the game.*

Below: *Cornerback Ryan Smith pounces on a Utah State fumble. The Utes forced three turnovers in the contest.*

GAME 3 RECAP

Aggies	0	0	6	0	– 6
UTES	20	21	7	0	– 48

UTAH – Paris Warren 4 run
(Bryan Borreson kick) 10:49, 1st
UTAH – Marty Johnson 1 run
(Borreson kick) 2:08, 1st
UTAH – Alex Smith 7 run
(Borreson kick failed) 0:15, 1st
UTAH – Quinton Ganther 2 run
(Borreson kick) 8:08, 2nd
UTAH – Paris Warren 10 pass from Smith
(Borreson kick) 3:29, 2nd
UTAH – Jonathan Fanene 76 interception return
(Dan Beardall kick) 1:25, 2nd
UTAH STATE – Richards 8 pass from Cox
(pass failed) 7:07, 3rd
UTAH – John Madsen 6 pass from Brian Johnson
(Beardall kick) 3:50, 3rd

UTAH	Final Statistics	Utah State
21	First Downs	18
221	Net Rushing	48
220	Passing Yards	247
441	Total Offense	295
28:07	Time of Possession	31:53

SCOTT G. WINTERTON

TOM SMART

SCOTT G. WINTERTON

TOM SMART

HODGE
49

Opposite: *Marty Johnson goes over the top for one of his record-tying four touchdowns as Utah topped Air Force in its Mountain West Conference opener.*

Right: *Utah defensive end Marquess Ledbetter pulls down Air Force quarterback Shaun Carney during the Utes' homecoming victory at Rice-Eccles Stadium.*

GAME 4: Utah 49, Air Force 35

Saturday, September 25, 2004: Salt Lake City

	AP TOP 25	ESPN/USA TODAY	BCS
SEPTEMBER 26	14	14	n/a

TOM SMART

Utes rally from a 14-0 deficit to prevail in homecoming game against Air Force. Tailback Marty Johnson ties a school record with four rushing touchdowns.

As Urban Meyer walked off the field at Rice-Eccles Stadium, he was congratulated by a well-wisher who said the 14th-ranked Utes' 49-35 homecoming win over Air Force was a bit "ugly."

The commentary didn't sit well.

"That was one of the prettiest wins I've ever been a part of," said Meyer. "We just beat Air Force and scored 49 points on them."

Utah's highest point total in nearly three years came in a 3 1/2-hour contest featuring a combined 976 yards of offense, 46 first downs and 21 third-down conversions. For the Utes, it also included a rally from a 14-0 deficit.

"That was a great win," continued Meyer. "That was a fantastic win offensively and defensively."

Marty Johnson scored three of his school record-tying four touchdowns rushing in the second half as the Utes

TOM SMART

Top Right: *A Utah fan proudly displays his choice of candidates for the Heisman Trophy.*

Bottom Right: *Utah defensive backs Bo Nagahi and Ryan Smith double up to force Air Force into an incompletion.*

Below: *Linebacker Spencer Toone and safety Eric Weddle teamed for a tackle in the Utes' 49-35 victory over Air Force.*

TOM SMART

TOM SMART

MITCH DUMKE

managed to hold off the pesky Falcons and win their Mountain West Conference opener. At 4-0 overall, they're off to their best start since 1994 and extended their winning streak to eight games over two seasons.

Air Force, meanwhile, suffered its first loss in Salt Lake City since 1995.

"It's good to have them in the rear-view mirror, I'll tell you that. They fight and fight," said safety Morgan Scalley. "I'll tell you what, they tested our will. They tested our character and you saw a Utah team out there that was fighting and fighting to the end."

The Utes had to. As was the case in last year's triple-overtime win and the loss in Utah the year before, the Falcons kept coming back.

A key play late in the third quarter, though, wound up reducing the threat significantly - if not, permanently.

With the Utes clinging to a 35-28 lead, defensive lineman Marquess Ledbetter recovered an Air Force fumble on the Falcon 42. Steve Fifita jarred the ball away from quarterback Shaun Carney on a play that took officials quite a bit of time to sort out.

"I guess the refs didn't have time to see what happened but I saw it. I was watching the whole time," said Ledbetter, who scooped the ball up after it landed on the ground between Fifita's legs. "I just grabbed it before the Air Force players got to it. It was a legit fumble."

The turnover ushered in a Utah scoring drive that put the game out of reach early in the fourth quarter. Johnson capped the six-play series with a two-yard touchdown run. He added a one-yard score when the Utes got the ball again as the margin spread to 21 points for the second time in the half. Air Force's lone retaliation was a touchdown with 22 seconds remaining.

"The officials didn't beat us. We had good opportunities in the game," said AFA coach Fisher DeBerry. "Our guys didn't quit. We had a chance to win but we didn't make the plays when we needed to."

The Utes scored touchdowns on their first two possessions of the second half - on a 13-yard pass from Alex Smith to Steve Savoy and on an 8-yard run by Johnson - complete a decisive 35-0 burst over the second and third quarters.

"They schemed us well and had some success early on," said Smith, who completed 13 passes for 260 yards and two touchdowns. "It was hard to anticipate what they were going to do. We had to get a feel for them at the beginning."

A couple of Utah streaks came to an end in the first half when Air Force jumped out to a 14-0 advantage - the largest hole the Utes have been in since last October's 47-35 loss to New Mexico.

Carney's early 5-yard touchdown run not only put the Falcons ahead, it also snapped a string of nine straight games in which the Utes had scored first. The score also left them trailing for the first time in six contests.

Carney compounded Utah's woes less than four minutes into the second quarter when he scampered 47 yards for another touchdown. At the time, Air Force had converted on 5-of-7 third-down situations.

Meyer said the situation caused a little panic on the Ute sideline.

"I wish I could say it was calm, cool and we knew it was going to work out like this," he said.

Defensive coordinator Kyle Whittingham told Meyer it took the

The Ute Marching Band played the national anthem as Air Force jets flew over the stadium.

TOM SMART

Utes awhile to adjust to the speed of the game. Offensively, Meyer said that the Falcons did things to keep them off track. Adjustments were made, however, and things eventually turned around.

"I think everybody remained calm," said Utah linebacker Spencer Toone, who finished with a game-high 14 tackles. "But it was just like, man, we've got to step it up."

Trailing 14-0, the Utes began their successful rally with an eight-play, 79-yard scoring drive. A 2-yard touchdown run by Johnson put them on the board until a late flurry produced two more scores.

With 2:37 remaining in the half, Smith and Paris Warren (who led Utah with six receptions) teamed on a 65-yard scoring strike. It evened the score, but only for 43 seconds.

On Air Force's next play from scrimmage, Utah cornerback Ryan Smith forced running back Anthony Butler to fumble. Toone recovered it on the Falcon 21 to set up the go-ahead score. Two rushes by Smith, the second covering 11 yards and aided by a goal-line block by Steve Savoy, resulted in a touchdown and put the Utes on top for good.

A 49-yard field goal attempt by Michael Greenaway was wide right as time expired, leaving Utah's lead at 21-14.

"We realized that we didn't need to panic. The option is something you really have to get used to within the first couple of series," said Scalley. "We felt like we did get a little grasp on it. Luckily, our offense came back and put up some points."

Top Left: Members of Utah's 1964 Liberty Bowl championship team were honored at halftime of the Homecoming win over Air Force.

Top Right: Wide receiver Steve Savoy picks up yardage after making a catch as the Utes rallied to defeat Air Force.

Below Left: The nationally ranked Utes take the field for Homecoming. Utah overcame an early 14-0 deficit to defeat Air Force convincingly.

Below Right: A young Utes fan.

GAME 4 RECAP

Falcons	7	7	14	7	– 35
UTES	0	21	14	14	– 49

AFA – Carney 5 run
(Greenaway kick) 11:13, 1st

AFA – Carney 47 run
(Greenaway kick), 11:43, 2nd

UTAH – Marty Johnson 2 run
(Bryan Borreson kick) 9:43, 2nd

UTAH – Paris Warren 65 pass from Alex Smith
(Borreson kick) 2:37, 2nd

UTAH – Smith 10 run
(Borreson kick) 1:54, 2nd

UTAH – Steve Savoy 13 pass from Smith
(Borreson kick) 12:15, 3rd

UTAH – M. Johnson
(Borreson kick) 8:40, 3rd

AFA – Stahr 6 pass from Carney
(Greenaway kick) 5:28, 3rd

AFA – Carney 2 run
(Greenaway kick) 2:14, 3rd

UTAH – M. Johnson 2 run
(Borreson kick) 12:51, 4th

UTAH – M. Johnson 1 run
(Borreson kick) 7:30, 4th

AFA – Moss 5 run
(Eberle kick) 0:22, 4th

Air Force	Final Statistics	UTAH
21	First Downs	25
302	Net Rushing	245
169	Passing Yards	260
471	Total Offense	505
34:33	Time of Possession	25:27

TOM SMART

MITCH DUMKE

UTAH
1

Opposite: Marty Johnson sets up a Utah touchdown with this long run in the win at New Mexico. He rushed for 99 yards on 11 carries in the contest.

Right: Utah nose guard Steve Fifita makes a tackle during a dominating performance by the Utes. The Lobos managed just 157 yards and eight first downs in the game.

GAME 5: Utah 28, New Mexico 7

Friday, October 1, 2004: Albuquerque, N.M.

	AP TOP 25	ESPN/USA TODAY	BCS
OCTOBER 3	11	11	n/a
OCTOBER 10	11	10	n/a

RAVELL CALL

The Utes avenge a 2003 loss at home by overpowering the Lobos in New Mexico. Ten Utah defenders make tackles behind the line of scrimmage.

ALBUQUERQUE, N.M. - This time, Utah left the Land of Enchantment smiling.

Led by a defense that limited New Mexico to just 157 yards and eight first downs, the 14th-ranked Utes avenged past troubles against the Lobos with a convincing 28-7 victory at University Stadium.

"Our guys were on a mission this week," said Utah defensive coordinator Kyle Whittingham. "They had something to prove. They were ticked off after last season."

Revenge proved to be sweet for the Utes, who improved to 5-0 overall (their best start since 1994) and 2-0 in Mountain West Conference play. They've now won nine straight games dating back to last season and eight consecutive on the road. Utah hasn't lost since falling to New Mexico last season in Salt Lake City.

Defensive end Marquess Ledbetter, one of 10 Utes to make a tackle behind the line of scrimmage, said the

RAVELL CALL

Top Right: *Utah players sing the school song in front a group of fans who made the trip to New Mexico. The win avenged a setback in Salt Lake City a year earlier.*

Bottom Right: *Alex Smith is congratulated by Steve Savoy after scoring a touchdown in Albuquerque.*

Below: *Quarterback Alex Smith unloads a pass as offensive lineman Makai Aalona looks on. Smith led an offense that racked up 24 first downs and 466 yards against New Mexico's famed defense.*

RAVELL CALL

RAVELL CALL

RAVELL CALL

team, as a whole, was determined to get the job done.

"We weren't going to let up like we did last year," said Ledbetter. "We were going to come out and dominate for four quarters."

And it all began up front, where Utah's defense faced a beefy New Mexico line whose average size was 6-foot-5 and 326 pounds.

"That's what we had to come out and do," said defensive tackle Sione Pouha. "Those are some big guys. Probably the best offensive line we are going to play in the Mountain West."

The Lobos (2-3, 0-1), who played with injured running back DonTrell Moore, never mounted much of a threat offensively. Their highly touted defense was also ineffective. Utah wound up with 466 yards of total offense and 24 first downs. The Utes had 278 yards rushing, becoming just the third team in 50 games to surpass 200 against the Lobos.

"I think it all started on the opening kickoff," said Utah coach Urban Meyer. "When we play as well as we do on special teams and defense, and the offense scores in the red zone, we've got a good team."

Steve Savoy's 10-yard touchdown run midway through the fourth quarter capped all scoring in a contest all but officially decided in the first half.

After opening with six straight pass plays, Utah switched to the run and it quickly paid off. Marty Johnson followed a short rush with a 59-yarder to set up the game's first score. Alex Smith's 3-yard touchdown run put the Utes on top early.

The 7-0 lead held firm for nearly 7 1/2 minutes until the Lobos pulled even on a 68-yard fumble return by cornerback Gabriel Fulbright. He scooped up the ball after it fell to the ground on what appeared to be an incomplete pass by Smith, who was hit on the play by New Mexico linebacker Mike Mohoric.

Utah retaliated by scoring two touchdowns on lengthy drives to secure a 21-7 lead by the time the first half was complete. Both second-quarter scores came on the ground, where it took the Utes less than 17 minutes to outrush each of New Mexico's four previous opponents this year - eclipsing Oregon State's 124 yards rushing in a 17-7 win over the Lobos on September 18.

A 7-yard run by Paris Warren opened the decisive scoring stretch and capped off the Utes' fifth scoring drive of 80 or more yards this season.

Punter Matt Kovacevich kept the next Utah possession alive when he ran 21 yards on fourth-and-14 from the Ute 20.

"Right when I got on the edge I was about to kick it," he said. "I saw that first-down marker was open and I just went for it."

Two other first downs followed before Smith ran six yards for his second touchdown of the night.

Besides a commanding lead at the break, the Utes were dominant statistically - despite losing two fumbles. They held a big advantage in first downs (17-4), total offensive yardage (323-92) and tackles for loss (8-2). Utah converted on six of its nine third-down situations, while denying New Mexico seven times.

"It was execution. We ran the same plays we ran last week," said New Mexico coach Rocky Long. "They worked pretty good last week but didn't work very well this week. That's a combination of not executing and their defense being pretty good."

Starting safety Morgan Scalley, who intercepted a pass, said it was even more than that.

"We felt like we were the better prepared team and we showed it tonight," he said.

Utah running back Quinton Ganther ran for a game-high 106 yards as the Utes prevailed in a meeting between the Mountain West's best offense and top-rated defense.

RAVELL CALL

RAVELL CALL

GAME 5 RECAP

UTES	7	14	0	7	– 28
Lobos	7	0	0	0	– 7

UTAH – Alex Smith 3 run
(Bryan Borreson kick) 7:34, 1st
NM – Fulbright 68 fumble return
(Zunker kick) 0:10, 1st
UTAH – Paris Warren 7 run
(Borreson kick) 12:14, 2nd
UTAH – Smith 6 run
(Borreson kick) 4:42, 2nd
UTAH – Steve Savoy 10 run
(Borreson kick) 9:06, 4th

UTAH	Final Statistics	New Mexico
24	First Downs	8
278	Net Rushing	74
188	Passing Yards	83
466	Total Offense	157
35:39	Time of Possession	24:21

RAVELL CALL

Above: *Linebacker Tommy Hackenbruck makes one of his three tackles-for-loss as the Utah defense set the tone at New Mexico.*

Right: *Reza Williams makes a tackle against the Lobos.*

RAVELL CALL

RAVELL CALL

__Top Left:__ Defensive coordinator Kyle Whittingham had the Utes fired up at University Stadium.

__Top Right:__ Utah fans were happy campers in the Land of Enchantment.

__Below:__ Utah wide receiver Steve Savoy is tackled after a long gain against New Mexico.

RAVELL CALL

XEROX
WELLS FARGO
UTAH
48
55
41
90

Opposite: *Offensive lineman Andrew Johnson, special teams standout Grady Marshall and defensive tackle Sione Pouha lead the postgame celebration following Utah's impressive win over North Carolina.*

Right: *Utah linebacker Spencer Toone makes one of his nine stops as the Utes overpowered the visiting Tar Heels.*

TOM SMART

GAME 6: Utah 46, North Carolina 16

Saturday, October 16, 2004: Salt Lake City

	AP TOP 25	ESPN/USA TODAY	BCS
OCTOBER 17	9	10	7

TOM SMART

A whopping 669 yards of total offense and 35 first downs lifts the Utes to an easy victory in their first game against an ACC opponent.

With Carolina no longer on its mind, undefeated Utah finds itself like a promising candidate on election night.

Facing one of the nation's lowest-ranked defenses, they racked up 669 yards of total offense - the second-highest tally in school history - and 35 first downs.

Saturday's 46-16 win over North Carolina closed what Utah hopes will be a successful campaign for respect in this season's first Bowl Championship Series rankings.

Though results won't be revealed until Monday, the Utes (6-0) are in prime position for good news. They entered the week ranked 10th in the ESPN/USA Today coaches poll and 11th in the Associated Press Top 25 and have now won 10 straight games over the past two seasons.

***Top Right:** Back-up quarterback Brian Johnson completed two passes for 40 yards in the rout over North Carolina.*

***Bottom Right:** Utah fans celebrate after the Utes prevailed in their first-ever meeting against an ACC team.*

***Below:** Middle linebacker Tommy Hackenbruck helped Utah bring down North Carolina at Rice-Eccles Stadium.*

MITCH DUMKE

TOM SMART

TOM SMART

The latest triumph came before the fourth-largest crowd in Rice-Eccles Stadium history. A packed house of 45,319 provided an enthusiastic atmosphere for the would-be BCS busters.

Led by quarterback Alex Smith and wide receiver Steve Savoy, the Utes improved to 5-1 against BCS schools under coach Urban Meyer with a convincing win in their first game against an Atlantic Coast Conference opponent.

"I was very impressed with how our offense played tonight," said Meyer. "Alex really played well and our offensive line allowed him to sit back there and pick them apart. That was really the first time we've been able to do that."

Smith, now 15-1 as Utah's starter, threw for 341 yards (topping 300 for the third time in his career) and four touchdowns before giving way to backup Brian Johnson early in the fourth quarter. He completed 10 passes to Savoy, who wound up with 154 yards receiving and a score. The sophomore also rushed for 54 yards, one less than Smith.

"For the offense to come out there and perform the way we did was great," said Smith. "We spread the ball around and did so many things well. We really hit full stride."

Savoy, a former North Carolina recruit, backed up comments earlier in the week that he wanted to show the Tar Heels (3-4) that they missed out on something special.

It was one of several messages delivered on a night when the visitors lost eight players to injury, including quarterback Darian Durant, who sprained his right elbow.

The Utes added to a 20-point halftime lead by outscoring the Tar Heels 16-7 in the second half. A 5-yard run by Smith and a 15-yard pass to John Madsen produced touchdowns that preceded a team safety created when Grady Marshall blocked a punt late in the game.

Carolina surprised Utah by opening the game with a sustained scoring drive. The Tar Heels converted on third down twice and fourth down once while marching 59 yards on 11 plays to take a 7-0 advantage less than six minutes into the contest. Running back Madison Hedgecock capped the series with the first of two 1-yard touchdown runs he had in the game - the second came in the third quarter.

Trailing for just the second time this season, Utah responded with a flurry before the half was complete. The Utes led 30-10 at the intermission after racking up 396 yards of total offense.

The defense got things kick-started after Utah's first possession ended with four plays and a punt. Marquess Ledbetter forced a North Carolina fumble and Spencer Toone recovered it to give the Utes possession on the Tar Heel 29.

Smith and Savoy prevented another stalled drive by teaming on a 23-yard pass play on third down. Marty Johnson followed with a 1-yard run as Utah pulled even midway through the first quarter. Bryan Borreson later added a 22-yard field goal - his ninth-straight successful kick over two seasons - to make it 10-7.

The margin swelled in the second quarter when Smith fired three touchdown passes for Utah, while UNC managed just a 29-yard field goal by Connor

__Right:__ Utah defenders Kite Afeaki and Marquess Ledbetter celebrate after making a stop against North Carolina.

MITCH DUMKE

Barth. Quinton Ganther's 5-yard reception opened the outburst, which ended with a 46-yard scoring strike to Savoy and a 6-yard TD catch by Paris Warren.

The latter came with only 1.8 seconds remaining in the half. It ended a 99-yard drive by the Utes that featured 10 plays and took less than two minutes to complete.

Smith powered the sequence by completing 6-of-7 passes for 67 yards. He also rushed for 32 yards on three carries.

TOM SMART

Above: Spencer Toone is congratulated by teammate Tommy Hackenbruck after recovering a fumble in Utah's 30-point win over North Carolina.

GAME 6 RECAP

Tar Heels	7	3	6	0	– 16
UTES	10	20	7	9	– 46

NC – Hedgecock 1 run (Barth kick) 9:15, 1st

UTAH – Marty Johnson 6 run (Bryan Borreson kick) 6:42, 1st

UTAH – Borreson 22 FG, 0:58, 1st

UTAH – Quinton Ganther 5 pass from Alex Smith (Borreson kick) 13:39, 2nd

NC – Barth 29 FG, 9:45, 2nd

UTAH – Steve Savoy 46 pass from Smith (Borreson kick) 7:50, 2nd

UTAH – Paris Warren 6 pass from Smith (Borreson kick failed) 0:02, 2nd

UTAH – Smith 5 run (Carroll kick) 10:17, 3rd

NC – Hedgecock 1 run (rush no good) 1:57, 3rd

UTAH – John Madsen 15 pass from Smith (Carroll kick), 12:30, 4th

UTAH – Team safety, 6:44, 4th

North Carolina	Final Statistics	UTAH
14	First Downs	35
66	Net Rushing	301
173	Passing Yards	381
221	Total Offense	669
24:46	Time of Possession	35:14

PAGE 43

Top Left: *Utah's speedy return specialist Justin Walker brought this North Carolina kickoff back 27 yards.*

Top Right: *Utah head coach Urban Meyer and defensive line coach Gary Andersen celebrate after the Utes make a goal-line stand.*

Below: *Running back Quinton Ganther dives over the goal line for a touchdown on a 5-yard pass play from Alex Smith in the North Carolina game.*

MITCH DUMKE

TOM SMART

TOM SMART

Opposite: *After taking a hand-off from Bo Nagahi, Morgan Scalley returned the opening kickoff against UNLV 90 yards for a touchdown.*

Right: *Utah's John Madsen celebrates as Utah beats UNLV 52-21 at Rice-Eccels Stadium.*

GAME 7: Utah 63, UNLV 28

Saturday, October 23, 2004: Salt Lake City

	AP TOP 25	ESPN/USA TODAY	BCS
OCTOBER 24	9	10	6

TOM SMART

Rain fails to dampen Utah's point parade. After rout, Rebels coach John Robinson says Utes are national championship-caliber team.

It rained, but not on Utah's parade Saturday at Rice-Eccles Stadium.

The ninth-ranked Utes poured it on quickly and often in a 63-28 victory over UNLV.

They returned the opening kickoff for a touchdown and scored on their first play from scrimmage in a record-tying and decisive start. The outburst fueled what wound up being the Utes' highest point total since a 66-point outburst against Idaho State in 1994.

"I think it was a great team effort," head coach Urban Meyer said after Utah scored six touchdowns on offense, two on special teams and one on defense. Kicker David Carroll tied a team record with nine PATs.

"Utah is a potential national championship-caliber team," said UNLV coach John Robinson. "Some people will question that, but they are playing good football and are as good as any team in the nation."

TOM SMART

Top Right: *Utah fans found many a reason to stay active despite the rain as the Utes overpowered UNLV.*

Bottom Right: *Utah defenders ganged up on UNLV. The Utes stopped the Rebels on third down 10 times.*

Below: *Freshman kicker David Carroll tied a school record in his first start by making all nine of his extra-point attempts.*

TOM SMART

TOM SMART

TOM SMART

The Utes, who have now won 11 traight games over two seasons, scored 8 points in the first quarter, equaling a chool-record previously matched three imes (1969, 1983, 1997).

Morgan Scalley opened the outburst with a 90-yard kickoff return. Bo Nagahi ielded it deep in the end zone and ran t to the 10-yard line before handing it off on a reverse to Scalley, who rambled down a wide-open right sideline. Though several UNLV defenders wound up giving chase, he managed to cap Jtah's first 100-yard return for a score n 19 years.

"Special teams did great tonight. We ove that. It's a big part of the game," said Nagahi. "There was no better way o start the game than with Morgan's ouchdown. It gave us a lot of momen-um."

Just more than three minutes after Scalley's score, the Utes crossed the goal ine again after Grady Marshall blocked a punt for the second consecutive week. Derrek Richards recovered it on the JNLV 27, where Alex Smith teamed with Steve Savoy on a touchdown pass.

Utah led 14-0 despite having the ball or just 24 seconds.

Following a missed field goal by the Rebels, the Utes embarked upon a engthy scoring drive. An 18-yard scor-ng strike from Smith to Travis LaTendresse provided the finishing ouch on an eight-play, 76-yard equence.

Trailing 21-0, UNLV fired back with its irst score. A 4-yard touchdown by Dyante Perkins put the Rebels on the board near the end of the quarter. It was overshadowed, though, by Utah's esponse. With just 24 seconds remain-ng, Smith ran 70 yards for a score. He olled to the left before cutting and eluding several would-be tacklers. Savoy had a key block on the longest run of Smith's career.

Smith, who finished with 147 yards passing and 77 yards rushing before being replaced by backup Brian Johnson late in the third quarter, praised Savoy, the offensive line and a fake by running back Quinton Ganther for setting up the score.

The Utes maintained their momentum on UNLV's ensuing possession when defensive end Jonathan Fanene recov-ered a fumble inside Rebel territory. Less than a minute into the second quarter, a 29-yard touchdown run by Savoy increased Utah's lead to 28 points.

An exchange of touchdowns followed before the half was complete. UNLV scored on a 38-yard run by Dominique Dorsey before Utah countered with a 9-yard scoring strike from Smith to Paris Warren to make it 42-14.

The halftime break failed to cool the Utes down. Though most of the 40,341 fans opted to head home because of the soggy weather, those who remained had several opportunities to cheer.

Utah extended its advantage to 63-21 in the third quarter by intercepting two passes, recovering a fumble and block-ing another punt.

Defensive tackle Steve Fifita's 6-yard interception return for a touchdown sparked the barrage. It preceded a 28-yard run by Dorsey in UNLV's failed bid to climb back into contention. The Utes followed with a 2-yard touchdown run by Marty Johnson and Shaun Harper's end-zone recovery of a blocked punt by "Utah Man" Billy Kinsey.

The fourth quarter passed quietly

Right: *Wide receiver Travis LaTendresse and quarter-back Alex Smith celebrate after teaming up on an 18-yard touchdown pass in the first quarter.*

MICHAEL BRANDY

- UNLV quarterback Shane Steichen's 25-yard TD run was the lone score - as the clock ran and the rain continued to fall.

It failed to dampen an impressive performance by the Utes, who entered the contest ranked seventh in the BCS standings, ninth in the AP Top 25 and 10th in the ESPN/USA Today coaches poll.

"We're very proud of our guys. We had three scores outside of offense," said Meyer. "Our players are terrific. The head coach gets too much credit. The guys on this team are responsible for the leadership and focus."

TOM SMART

Defensive coordinator Kyle Whittingham shouts instructions during Utah's lopsided win over UNLV in the rain at Rice-Eccles Stadium.

GAME 7 RECAP

Rebels	**7**	**7**	**7**	**7**	**- 28**
UTES	**21**	**14**	**21**	**0**	**- 63**

UTAH – Morgan Scalley 90 kickoff return (David Carroll kick) 14:45, 1st
UTAH – Steve Savoy 27 pass from Alex Smith (Carroll kick) 11:40, 1st
UTAH – Travis LaTendresse 18 pass from Smith (Carroll kick) 4:25, 1st
UNLV – Perkins 4 run (Aguayo kick) 1:49, 1st
UTAH – Smith 70 run (Carroll kick) 0:24, 1st
UTAH – Savoy 28 run (Carroll kick) 14:07, 2nd
UNLV – Dorsey 38 run (IAguayo kick) 6:44, 2nd
UTAH – Paris Warren 9 pass from Smith (Carroll kick) 0:21, 2nd
UTAH – Steve Fifita 6 interception return (Carroll kick) 10:49, 3rd
UNLV – Dorsey 28 run (Aguayo kick) 8:05, 3rd
UTAH – Marty Johnson 2 run (Carroll kick) 2:23, 3rd
UTAH – Shaun Harper 0 blocked FG (Carroll kick) 0:15, 3rd
UNLV – Steichen 25 run (Aguayo kick) 6:00, 4th

UNLV	Final Statistics	UTAH
17	First Downs	23
311	Net Rushing	281
111	Passing Yards	152
422	Total Offense	433
30:25	Time of Possession	29:35

PAGE 49

Top Left: *Utah defenders surround nose guard Steve Fifita after he scored a touchdown on a 6-yard interception return midway through the UNLV game.*

Top Right: *Running back Joe Johnson was among several reserves who saw extensive action in the fourth quarter. Utah led UNLV by 42 points after three quarters.*

Below: *Fans at Rice-Eccles Stadium braved cool, wet weather as the Utes rolled past UNLV.*

TOM SMART

HEIDA SMART

TOM SMART

SAN DIEGO STATE
SAN DIEGO STATE
UTAH
MOUNTAIN WEST

Opposite: *Running back Quinton Ganther runs past a pair of San Diego State defenders. The junior college transfer rushed for 45 yards in Uthah's victory at Qualcomm Stadium.*

Right: *Alex Smith prepares to throw.*

GAME 8: Utah 51, San Diego State 28

Saturday, October 30, 2004: San Diego, CA

	AP TOP 25	ESPN/USA TODAY	BCS
OCTOBER 31	7	8	6

TOM SMART

A successful homecoming for Helix High alum Alex Smith. He throws a career-high five touchdown passes in Utah's victory over the Aztecs.

SAN DIEGO - San Diego State's homecoming was nothing compared to that of Utah quarterback Alex Smith. The junior, who attended nearby Helix High, threw a career-high five touchdown passes in leading the Utes to a 51-28 victory over the Aztecs at Qualcomm Stadium.

It provided the Heisman Trophy candidate with some redemption in front of family and friends. Two years ago, he made a shaky collegiate debut here that included an interception and just two completions for four yards.

This time, Smith completed 22 passes for 298 yards in carrying the ninth-ranked Utes to their 12th straight win over two seasons - the second-longest streak in program history. It also extended a school record of victories at road or neutral sites to nine games.

"Obviously, it's very different in multiple ways," said Smith, who called his previous visit home a low point for

TOM SMART

Top Right: Utah defenders Jonathan Fanene and Tommy Hackenbruck enjoy the action from the bench while the offense was on the field in San Diego.

Bottom Right: Kyle Brady is backed by plenty of teammates in impeding the progress of a San Diego State runner.

Below: Tommy Hackenbruck makes a stop as the Utes topple San Diego State.

TOM SMART

TOM SMART

TOM SMART

both himself and the program. "It's the extreme opposite now. This is a special team."

At 8-0 overall and 4-0 in Mountain West Conference play, Utah is poised to move up from the sixth spot in the Bowl Championship Series standings, as well as the national rankings, thanks to upset losses suffered by Florida State and Miami.

The Utes are now 16-1 with Smith as their starter. He wasted little time setting the tone in the latest triumph.

Utah converted on third down six times while building a 34-21 halftime lead. Smith led the offense by completing 16 of 24 passes for 218 yards and four touchdowns.

It almost wasn't enough, however, as SDSU proved to be pesky.

With 3:37 remaining in the first half, the Aztecs closed the gap to 24-21 when defensive tackle Blake Lobel returned a John Madsen fumble 19 yards for a touchdown.

The Utes, though, responded with a late flurry to regain some breathing room and maintain a lead they held since their first possession. A 36-yard field goal by David Carroll and a 3-yard scoring strike from Smith to Travis LaTendresse squelched the threat.

The latter, which came with two seconds remaining, was set up by a blocked punt. Blake Burdette deflected the kick and Tim Harris pounced on it.

"Momentum is a big deal," said Utah coach Urban Meyer. "I thought that was the checkmate of the game."

Utah added to the outburst early in the third quarter by scoring on its opening series.

Morgan Scalley's 32-yard kickoff return gave the Utes good field position. They eventually cashed in on it when Marty Johnson ran four yards for a touchdown.

Utah's 41-21 lead held firm until the fourth quarter when SDSU's Jeff Webb hauled in a 21-yard pass from quarterback Kevin O'Connell.

It proved inconsequential as the Utes fired back twice down the stretch to cap all scoring in the contest, which broke an 11-11-1 tie in the all-time series. A 20-yard touchdown pass from Smith to Steve Savoy was followed by a 23-yard field goal by Carroll.

Utah built a 10-0 lead in the first quarter, a good omen considering SDSU entered the game with an 0-12 mark under third-year coach Tom Craft when trailing early.

A 5-yard touchdown pass from Smith to Paris Warren got things started. It capped a 12-play, 61-yard drive that took 4:51 off the clock. The Utes later added a 27-yard field goal by Carroll. Between scores, Scalley blocked a 40-yard attempt by Garrett Palmer of the Aztecs. By game's end, the Utah senior also recorded an interception.

SDSU scored its first points early in the second quarter on a 29-yard touchdown pass from O'Connell to Webb.

Utah retaliated quickly. Just 34 seconds passed before Smith and Warren teamed up for a 10-yard score to make it 17-7. A 58-yard throw from Smith to John Madsen, along with a face-mask penalty on the Aztecs, fueled the fast sequence.

Wide receiver Steve Savoy brings in one of his two touchdown catches in Utah's Mountain West Conference victory at San Diego State.

TOM SMART

A pair of sustained drives, one by each team, followed. A 5-yard run by O'Connell capped a 10-play, 72-yard march by SDSU. An 18-yard TD throw from Smith to Savoy provided the finale on an 11-play, 69-yard series by the Utes.

TOM SMART

Above: *A large contingent of Utah fans made the journey to San Diego for the game. They didn't leave disappointed.*

GAME 8 RECAP

UTES	10	24	7	10	– 51
Aztecs	0	21	0	7	– 28

UTAH – Paris Warren 5 pass from Alex Smith (David Carroll kick) 8:17, 1st
UTAH – Carroll 29 FG, 2:02, 1st
SDSU – Webb 9 pass from O'Connell (Palmer kick) 14:56, 2nd
UTAH – Warren 10 pass from Smith (Carroll kick) 14:22, 2nd
SDSU – O'Connell 5 run (Palmer kick) 11:24, 2nd
UTAH – Steve Savoy 18 pass from Smith (Carroll kick) 7:49, 2nd
SDSU – Lobel 19 fumble return (Palmer kick) 3:37, 2nd
UTAH – Carroll 36 FG, 1:14, 2nd
UTAH – Travis LaTendresse 3 pass from Smith (Carroll kick) 0:45, 2nd
UTAH – Marty Johnson 4 run (Carroll kick) 12:45, 3rd
SDSU – Webb 21 pass from O'Connell (Palmer kick) 14:51, 4th
UTAH – Steve Savoy 23 pass from Smith (Carroll kick) 13:12, 4th
UTAH – Carroll 23 FG, 8:26, 4th

UTAH	Final Statistics	SDSU
29	First Downs	23
173	Net Rushing	162
375	Passing Yards	252
548	Total Offense	414
33:05	Time of Possession	26:55

PAGE 55:
Top Left: *Quarterbacks coach Dan Mullen, defensive coordinator Kyle Whittingham and head coach Urban Meyer in the heat of battle in Utah's victory over San Diego State.*

Top Right: *Wide receiver Paris Warren runs past the Aztecs for one of two touchdowns he scored in the game.*

Below: *Shaun Harper celebrates after a Utah stop. The Utes held the Aztecs scoreless in the first and third quarters.*

TOM SMART

TOM SMART

TOM SMART

Opposite: Utah receiver Paris Warren dives into the end zone for a touchdown. He scored twice in the first quarter as the Utes routed the Rams.

Right: Coach Urban Meyer shouts instructions during the CSU game.

GAME 9: Utah 63, Colorado State 31

Saturday, November 6, 2004: Salt Lake City

	AP TOP 25	ESPN/USA TODAY	BCS
NOVEMBER 7	7	8	7

TOM SMART

Urban Meyer guides the seventh-ranked Utes to their first 9-0 start with a lopsided win over perennial Mountain West Conference power CSU.

Utah proved to be Ram-tough in securing its first 9-0 start to a season.

Heisman Trophy candidate Alex Smith completed 21-of-26 passes for 291 yards and four touchdowns as the seventh-ranked Utes rolled to a 63-31 victory over Colorado State.

"The best thing about a 9-0 start is the chance to go to 10-0," said Utah coach Urban Meyer. "Our first team played excellent. I think Alex is the best quarterback in college football."

They're now 18-1 with Smith as their starting quarterback and have won 13 consecutive games over two seasons. The scoring outburst lifted them from seventh to first in single-season point production with 412.

Utah rolled to a 42-3 lead late in the first half behind the play of Smith and safety Morgan Scalley.

"We came out and wanted to earn their respect and hopefully we did that," said Scalley. "We're playing for all

JEFFREY ALLRED

Top Right: *Utah defenders Ryan Smith and Corey Dodds break up a Colorado State pass play.*

Bottom Right: *Utah safety Morgan Scalley en route to a school-record 88-yard fumble recovery for a touchdown. He also had two interceptions in the game.*

Below: *Linebacker Spencer Toone makes one of his team-high 11 tackles in the overwhelming win over perennial league power Colorado State.*

TOM SMART

TOM SMART

TOM SMART

the past Utes, my dad included."

Smith connected on 14 passes for 152 yards and three scores over the first two quarters. He guided an offense that racked up 299 yards and 16 first downs during the decisive stretch.

A 5-yard touchdown pass from Smith to Paris Warren capped an opening drive that consisted of 12 plays and took a season-high 5:09 to complete. Less than two minutes later, Utah's lead doubled when Scalley returned a CSU fumble 88 yards for another score. His run down the left sideline set a new school record, eclipsing Arnold Parker's game-winning romp of 80 yards in last year's Ute win in Fort Collins.

Trailing 14-0, the Rams responded with a 39-yard field goal by Jeff Babcock.

It failed, however, to kick-start a momentum shift.

Before the opening quarter was complete, Utah fired back with its second 80-yard scoring drive. A 6-yard strike from Smith to Warren opened an outburst that produced four touchdowns before CSU's first trip to the end zone.

A 22-yard TD pass from Smith to Savoy preceded a pair of 1-yard scores by running back Marty Johnson as the Utes extended their lead to 39 points. A late touchdown by the Rams - with 12 seconds remaining on a 26-yard pass from Caleb Hanie to Damon Morton - made it 42-10 at halftime.

In the third quarter, Utah added short touchdown runs by Johnson (1 yard) and back-up quarterback Brian Johnson (4 yards) to take its biggest lead of the game at 56-10 after freshman kicker David Carroll made his 25th consecutive PAT. He wound up with 26 by game's end.

Both scores, along with the Utes' last touchdown in the first half, followed CSU turnovers - contributing to a tally that grew to five TDs by game's end. Scalley and fellow safety Eric Weddle provided the changes of possession. Scalley added two interceptions to his fumble recovery, while Weddle intercepted a pass and a recovered a fumble.

With the game well out of reach, CSU put three late touchdowns on the board to close the gap cosmetically. A 1-yard touchdown run by Marcus Houston, a 26-yard touchdown throw from Hanie to Damon Morton and a 44-yard run by Hanie.

Weary of seeing their deficit cut, the Utes reinserted Smith and he orchestrated a six-play, 77-yard drive that ended

Starting safety Eric Weddle recovered a fumble and picked off a psss as Utah's defense shut down visiting Colorado State.

TOM SMART

with a nine-yard TD pass to Warren. It provided the final margin of victory and helped up their final total offense tally to 534 yards.

TOM SMART

A sign by a Utah fan asks would-be suitors to look elsewhere for a head football coach. Urban Meyer's services, however, were highly sought after.

GAME 9 RECAP

Rams	3	7	0	21	– 31
UTES	21	21	14	7	– 63

UTAH – Paris Warren 5 pass from Alex Smith (David Carroll kick) 9:51, 1st
UTAH – Morgan Scalley 88 fumble return (Carroll kick) 8:04, 1st
CSU – Babcock, 39-field goal, 4:36, 1st
UTAH – Warren 6 pass from Smith (Carroll kick) 1:18, 1st
UTAH – Steve Savoy 22 pass from Smith (Carroll kick) 10:04, 2nd
UTAH – MartyJohnson 1 run (Carroll kick) 3:50, 2nd
UTAH – M. Johnson 1 run (Carroll) 0:39, 2nd
CSU – Morton 26 pass from Hanie (Babcock kick) 1:12, 2nd
UTAH – M. Johnson 1 run (Carroll kick), 9:14, 3rd
UTAH – Brian Johnson 4 run (Carroll kick) 5:43, 3rd
CSU – Houston 1 run (Babcock kick) 14:15, 4th
CSU – Morton 24 from Hanie (Babcock) 11:10, 4th
CSU – Hanie 48 run (Babcock kick) 7:15, 4th
UTAH – Warren 9 pass from Smith (Carroll kick) 5:07, 4th

CSU	Final Statistics	UTAH
23	First Downs	28
226	Net Rushing	242
194	Passing Yards	292
420	Total Offense	534
29:23	Time of Possession	30:37

Top Left: *Utah running back Marty Johnson works his way through the Colorado State defense. He scored a touchdown in the game.*

Top Right: *Defensive end Jonathan Fanene makes a stop while falling to the ground. Colorado State had just 10 points before a fourth-quarter surge.*

Below: *Tailback Quinton Ganther led all rushers with 81 yards. He carried the ball just seven times as the Utes continually seized opportunities.*

JEFFREY D. ALLRED

TOM SMART

JEFFREY D. ALLRED

A
B
0

Opposite: *The night the lights went out in Laramie. A power failure led to a near two-hour delay on a frigid night with the wind blowing in Wyoming. The Utes warmed up quickly by scoring all 45 of their points in the first three quarters.*

Right: *Utah head coach Urban Meyer makes his viewpoint known to an official during the Utes' victory over the Cowboys at War Memorial Stadium.*

GAME 10: Utah 45, Wyoming 28

Saturday, November 13, 2004: Laramie, WY

	AP TOP 25	ESPN/USA TODAY	BCS
NOVEMBER 14	5	6	6

AUGUST MILLER

A power outage delays a special night for the Utes. Once the lights come on, they clinch a second consecutive outright conference title for the first time in 51 years.

LARAMIE, Wyo. – A power outage delayed the start of Utah's 45-28 win over Wyoming on Saturday. It was nothing, however, compared to the wait that ended at the final horn.

The victory, coupled with BYU's loss to New Mexico earlier in the day, put an end to a lengthy drought for the Utes. For the first time in 51 years, they're back-to-back outright conference champions.

"We wanted to get it done tonight," said senior Morgan Scalley. "There was no postponement in our minds whatsoever."

It's the crown jewel of a growing list of accolades that includes 14 consecutive wins over two seasons and Utah's first 10-0 start.

Fans chanted "Beat BYU" as the Utes walked off the field. They'll host the Cougars Saturday at Rice-Eccles

AUGUST MILLER

Top Right: *Quinton Ganther fights for extra yardage against Wyoming on a cold, dark night in Larmine.*

Bottom Right: *Alex Smith is all smiles during a postgame interview with ESPN.*

Below: *Alex Smith and offensive lineman Tavo Tupola take time to celebrate Utah's title-clinching win at Wyoming. The Utes never trailed.*

AUGUST MILLER

AUGUST MILLER

AUGUST MILLER

Stadium.

"Teams that win conferences back-to-back are special," said Utah coach Urban Meyer, who received a Gatorade drenching late in the game. "But (we're) going to put that on hold for a week. Our focus is going to go on to one of the greatest rivalries in college football and that's next week."

Distractions were plentiful early on a cool night at War Memorial Stadium, where a blown transformer led to a delayed start.

"That was tough. That was Coaching 101. I kept looking through the manual and I couldn't find that-how to handle an hour-and-a half delay," said Meyer, who praised his staff and players for maintaining their composure.

The Utes, who spent much of the delay in a gym eating apples and oranges, extended their winning streak away from home to 10 games. They did so while becoming the most prolific single-season scoring team in school history-quickly surpassing the 14 points needed to top the 1994 mark of 426 points.

Utah never trailed while building a 31-7 halftime lead.

The Utes got things started by capitalizing on a pair of Wyoming turnovers. They scored touchdowns on their first two possessions after taking possession on a fumble recovery by Corey Dodds and an interception by Marquess Ledbetter.

Quarterback Alex Smith capped the first scoring drive with a 27-yard touchdown run. Marty Johnson added a 1-yard score 7 1/2 minutes later to make it 14-0.

Wyoming fired back with its only score of the half when a pass from quarterback Corey Bramlet caromed off of intended receiver Michael Ford and into the hands of Jovon Bouknight, who raced 59 yards down the left sideline to cut Utah's lead in half.

It didn't stay that way for long, though.

Before the first quarter was complete, the Utes concluded a 10-play drive with a 25-yard field goal by David Carroll.

It ushered in a run of 17 straight points by the Utes before the intermission. Less than two minutes after Carroll's kick, Scalley intercepted a pass to set up another touchdown by the Utes.

A 26-yard scoring strike from Smith to Paris Warren preceded a 10-yard touchdown pass to Steve Savoy before halftime.

The scores highlighted an impressive first half for Smith. The Heisman Trophy candidate completed 13-of-17 passes for 196 yards over the first two quarters.

With the game well out of reach, the Utes added two more touchdowns in the second half-off a 15-yard run by Savoy and a 15-yard pass from Smith to John Madsen. Between scores, Wyoming crossed the goal line on a 2-yard run by Bramlet.

The Cowboys produced two more touchdowns in the final 46 seconds-off a 1-yard run by Bramlet and a 20-yard pass from Bramlet to Bouknight-for a cosmetic finish.

"Hats off to our kids for not giving

Utah quarterback Alex Smith racked up 334 yards of total offense at Wyoming. He passed for 244 yards and ran for 90 more.

AUGUST MILLER

up," said Wyoming coach Joe Glenn. "We played hard and gave it all we had."

Utah's 17-point win continued a season-long streak of victories by 14 points or greater.

AUGUST MILLER

Utah wide receiver Steve Savoy fights his way into the end zone for a touchdown at Wyoming. He scored twice as the Utes claimed a second straight league title.

GAME 10 RECAP

UTES	17	14	14	0	– 45
Cowboys	7	0	7	14	– 28

UTAH – Alex Smith 27 run (David Carroll kick) 12:53, 1st

UTAH – Marty Johnson 1 run (Carroll kick) 5:30, 1st

WYO – Bouknight 59 pass from Bramlet (Yaussi kick) 3:39, 1st

UTAH – Carroll 25 FG, 0:14, 1st

UTAH – Paris Warren 26 pass from Smith (Carroll kick) 11:04, 2nd

UTAH – Steve Savoy 10 pass from Smith (Carroll kick) 4:08, 2nd

UTAH – Savoy 15 run (Carroll kick) 10:23, 3rd

WYO – Bramlet 2 run (Yaussi kick) 2:16, 3rd

UTAH – John Madsen 15 pass (Carroll kick) 0:00,3rd

WYO – Bramlet 1 run (Yaussi kick) 0:46, 4th

WYO – Bouknight 20 pass from Bramlet (Yaussi kick) 0:34, 1st

UTAH	Final Statistics	Wyoming
28	First Downs	23
244	Net Rushing	132
244	Passing Yards	278
488	Total Offense	410
30:29	Time of Possession	29:31

Top Left: *A power outage forced a delayed start of nearly two hours at aging War Memorial Stadium. Once the lights came on, the Utes proved to be even brighter.*

Top Right: *"Swoop" didn't fly south for the winter. The fair-feathered mascot joined many Utah fans in braving the cool, windy conditions in Wyoming.*

Below: *Utah running back Marty Johnson and tight end Blake Burdette celebrate after Johnson scored a touchdown in the first quarter.*

AUGUST MILLER

AUGUST MILLER

AUGUST MILLER

Utah
Urban!
Alex Smith
For

Opposite: *Fans storm the field at Rice-Eccles Stadium and tear down the goal posts after a 52-21 victory over arch rival BYU. The win gave the Utes their first 11-0 regular season.*

Right: *Utah receivers Steve Savoy and Paris Warren celebrate after one of Savoy's three touchdowns in the lopsided decision over BYU.*

GAME 11: Utah 52, BYU 21

Saturday, November 20, 2004: Salt Lake City

	AP TOP 25	ESPN/USA TODAY	BCS
NOVEMBER21	5	6	6
NOVEMBER 28	5	6	6
DECEMBER 5	5	6	6

TOM SMART

Fans storm the field at Rice-Eccles Stadium following historic victory over rival BYU. Utah finishes season 11-0 and is ticketed for Bowl Championship Series.

Utah cleared a path to the Bowl Championship Series with a 52-21 victory over BYU at Rice-Eccles Stadium. Saturday's victory gave the Utes their first 11-0 season.

"This is a dream come true for the team. I can't say enough about my teammates. They deserve this," said quarterback Alex Smith. "We are gonna get our shot to go to the BCS and play with the big boys."

Though not official until the final BCS standings are released on December 5, the fifth-ranked Utes are most likely headed to the Fiesta or Sugar bowls in January. They'll be the first team from a non-BCS conference to crash the financially lucrative system that was established in 1998.

TOM SMART

Top Right: *Utah defenders Reza Williams and Sione Pouha are all business while making a stop in the season-ending triumph against BYU.*

Bottom Right: *Middle linebacker Tommy Hackenbruck and safety Morgan Scalley join several teammates in celebrating a stop as Utah overpowered the Team Down South.*

Below: *A young Utah fan holds a sign that says it all. The undefeated Utes are headed to the Bowl Championship Series.*

MITCH DUMKE

MITCH DUMKE

TOM SMART

"I don't want to be overly dramatic but I think it's a historic day," said athletic director Chris Hill. "For a school like ours to earn our way into the biggest of bowls is absolutely fantastic."

A celebration ensued as hundreds of the 45,326 fans in attendance began pouring onto the field in the closing seconds. Many sported sombreros and tossed tortilla chips into the air (Tostitos is the Fiesta Bowl's chief sponsor) before tearing down the goal posts.

"What a great day for Salt Lake City," marveled Urban Meyer. "What a great day."

A trophy presentation at midfield, complete with defensive lineman Sione Pouha leading a group singing of the school song, enhanced the postgame festivities.

"I do believe that Utah is one of the top six teams in the country," Meyer said after the national broadcast on ESPN2. "We proved a point today on the field against a very good opponent."

BYU (5-6) could have become bowl eligible with a victory. The loss dropped the Cougars to 5-6 and gave them their third consecutive losing season, a first for the program in 40 years.

"I want to give Utah a lot of credit. They are an outstanding football team, so give them credit," said BYU coach Gary Crowton. "They represent the MWC very well and they have had a great season. I think they will represent the conference well, whoever they play, and will be very hard to beat."

Utah racked up 26 first downs and 538 yards of total offense in winning the Holy War for the third straight year. Smith completed 16-of-24 passes for 184 yards to lead an effective offense. Quinton Ganther finished with 122 yards rushing, while Paris Warren had a game-high eight receptions.

BYU quarterback John Beck was 17-of-32 passes for 213 yards and a pair of touchdowns. The Cougars wound up with 294 yards and 19 first downs.

"Alex threw two interceptions, which is very un-Alex like, but we played a very good defensive football team," said Meyer. "I think all three phases-offense, defense and kicking-did a great job. It was a complete football game."

If it weren't for one pivotal minute early in the third quarter, Utah's BCS hopes may have vanished into the cool autumn air.

Exactly 60 seconds separated two scores by the Utes that turned a slim lead into a comfortable advantage. A 40-yard field goal by David Carroll preceded Bo Nagahi's 12-yard fumble recovery for a touchdown that made the score 31-14.

Middle linebacker Tommy Hackenbruck created the latter by jarring the ball away from BYU receiver Antwaun Harris.

Though the Cougars responded quick-

Right: *Utah running back Marty Johnson celebrates during the Utes' 52-21 victory over BYU at Rice-Eccles Stadium.*

JEFFREY D. ALLRED

ly-on a 16-yard scoring strike from John Beck to Austin Collie-they would draw no closer the rest of the way. After an exchange of interceptions, Spencer White for BYU and Eric Weddle for Utah, the Utes scored a pair of touchdowns to take a 24-point lead into the final 10:34.

TOM SMART

Utah nose guard Steve Fifita dons a sombrero in the closing seconds of the BYU game. The Utes, as expected, were eventually invited to the Fiesta Bowl.

GAME 11 RECAP

Cougars	0	14	7	0	– 21
UTES	7	14	17	14	– 52

UTAH – Steve Savoy 2 run (David Carroll kick) 0:52, 1st
BYU – Watkins 5 pass from Beck (Payne kick) 12:13, 2nd
UTAH – Marty Johnson 5 run (Carroll kick) 9:28, 2nd
BYU – Brown 6 run (Payne kick) 5:40, 2nd
UTAH – Alex Smith 2 run (Carroll kick) 1:19, 2nd
UTAH – Carroll 30 FG, 11:43, 3rd
UTAH – Bo Nagahi 12 fumble return (Carroll kick) 10:43, 3rd
BYU – Collie 16 pass from Beck (Payne kick) 8:38, 3rd
UTAH – Savoy 92 run (Carroll kick), 5:59, 3rd
UTAH – Savoy 20 pass from Smith (Carroll kick) 10:34, 4th
UTAH – Steve Fifita 4 run (Carroll kick) 1:03, 4th

BYU	Final Statistics	UTAH
19	First Downs	26
81	Net Rushing	354
213	Passing Yards	184
294	Total Offense	538
23:39	Time of Possession	36:21

Top Left: *Steve Savoy's 92-yard touchdown run midway through the third quarter sparked a game-ending run of 21 unanswered points by the Utes.*

Top Right: *Former high school running back turned collegiate nose guard Steve Fifita rambled in for a four-yard touchdown run to cap all scoring in the contest.*

Below: *Utah fans were ready for a Fiesta Bowl invitation. Head coach Urban Meyer and the Utes were backed by sombreros and piniatas.*

TOM SMART

JEFFREY D. ALLRED

TOM SMART

Savoy opened the outburst with a 92-yard touchdown run down the right sideline. It was the second-longest ground score in Utah history, trailing only a Frank Nelson's 93-yarder against BYU in 1947. The Utes' next possession ended with a 20-yard touchdown pass from Smith to Savoy.

With just over a minute to go, defensive lineman and former high school running back Steve Fifita added a four-yard TD run to give the Utes their widest margin of victory over BYU since a 57-28 win in 1988.

Utah led 21-14 at halftime despite losing wide receiver Travis LaTendresse to a shoulder separation, Morgan Scalley to a migraine headache (he returned in the second half) and cornerback Gerald Fletcher to a knee injury. Though the Utes never trailed, Smith's first interception in 113 attempts prevented them from pulling away early in the second quarter.

It came on a fourth-and-7 play from the BYU 23 when Utah held a 14-7 lead. Nathan Soelberg picked it off for the Cougars and returned it 60 yards before being brought down by Smith. Two plays later, Curtis Brown rambled six yards for the tying touchdown.

JEFFREY ALLRED

Utah's Quinton Ganther leaps forward for part of his game-high 122 yards rushing. He did all his damage on just 11 carries.

TOM SMART

Utah cornerback Bo Nagahi scores a touchdown on as 12-yard fumble return early in the third quarter to extend the Utes' advantage to 31-14.

TOM SMART

TOM SMART

TOM SMART

TOM SMART

(Clockwise from Top Left) Head Coach Urban Meyer is given the traditional celebatory dousing towards the end of the BYU game.

Quarterback Alex Smith is carried off the field wearing a sombrero. The eventual Heisman Trophy finalist celebrates Utah's first 11-0 season.

The Utes, however, managed to regain the lead before the intermission thanks to a 12-play, 79-yard drive. The series featured a successful fake punt that Bo Nagahi kept alive with a 23-yard gain. Smith capped the sequence with a 2-yard touchdown run with just 1:19 remaining.

Utah's earlier scores came on short runs by Savoy and Marty Johnson. Between touchdowns, BYU ended a three-year touchdown drought against the Utes when John Beck teamed with Todd Watkins on a five-yard pass.

AUGUST MILLER

JEFFREY D. ALLRED

This Utah fan knew what it was time for.

AUGUST MILLER

Above: *Utah defensive linemen Sione Pouha and Reza Williams team up to bring down BYU quarterback John Beck. The Utes defeated the Cougars for the third consecutive year.*

Right: *Utah wide receiver Travis LaTendresse holds onto the ball after making a spectacular catch against BYU.*

TOM SMART

TOM SMART

TOM SMART

Bottom Left: *Marquess Ledbetter lowers the boom on a BYU ball carrier.*

Bottom Right: *Morgan Scalley breaks up another Cougar play.*

Above Left: *Linebacker Grady Marshall makes the tackle.*

Above Right: *Utah fans were out in full force for BYU.*

MITCH DUMKE

TOM SMART

TOM SMART

A sold-out Rice-Eccles Stadium versus BYU.

DON'T MUSS WITH US!
MUSS SEE T.V
GO UTES

TOM SMART

Opposite: ***Opposite:*** *The Mighty Utah Student Section, "The MUSS", set a standard of support unparalled in the Mountain West Conference.*

Right: *Workers hang a banner at Rice-Eccles Stadium letting everyone know this is the home of the Utes.*

GAME DAY Rice-Eccles Stadium

Record Crowds

JEFFREY D. ALLRED

Utah's record-setting season wasn't just confined to the football field. Rice-Eccles Stadium also got into the act.

Fans following the Utes arrived in record numbers as crowds averaged 44,112 over six home games – easily surpassing a one-year-old school record of 41,478 per outing. Three of the five biggest crowds in stadium history came through the turnstiles in 2004 as part of a strong schedule that featured visits by Texas A&M, Air Force, North Carolina, UNLV, Colorado State and BYU. Packed houses weren't the only

Top Right: "Swoop" leads the Utes onto the field.

Bottom Right: Ute players sing the school fight song, "Utah Man" after a victory at Rice-Eccles Staduim.

Below: A young Ute fan practices his cheers.

SSCOTT G. WINTERTON

SCOTT G. WINTERTON

TOM SMART

story line at the facility on the hill. The game day atmosphere was enhanced by loud, voisterous support of "The MUSS." Utah's student fan club was a familiar sight behind the Utah bench. They became such a vital part of the football team's success that a "MUSS" sticker was added to the back of the Utes' helmets this season. The Mighty Utah Student Section set a standard of support unparalleled in the Mountain West Conference. After each game, the football team joined the band and cheerleaders in front of the MUSS to sing "Utah Man," the school fight song. The new tradition caught on quickly and the chorus swelled as the season progressed. "To sing the fight song with us afterward, to see them stay involved, pumped and rowdy and loud – that's what college football is all about," quarterback Alex Smith told ESPN.com.

When the Utes closed out the regular season with a 52-21 win over arch rival BYU, thousands of fans ran onto the field and helped bring the goal posts down. It was a fitting finish to a perfect season at the scenic stadium. A national television audience got a firsthand view as ESPN's "College GameDay" program was broadcast from a temporary stage in the parking lot. Thousands of Utah fans attended the tapings Friday and Saturday. The Salt Lake City broadcast drew the show's highest ratings of the season. Lee Corso, one of GameDay's hosts, is featured on a color page inside Utah's media guide. "Rice-Eccles Stadium is as good as any place in the country,"

Right: "The MUSS" cheer on another score during a 2004 game.

TOM SMART

Below: *Utah fans show their support.*

TOM SMART

Top Left: *A Utah fan takes part in the time-honored tradition of face painting.*

Upper Right: *Lee Corso, Co-host of ESPN College Gameday says, "Rice-Eccles Stadium is as good as any place in the country."*

he said.

The home of the Utes underwent a $50 million renovation in 1998 and was used for the opening and closing ceremonies of the 2002 Winter Olympic Games. Its 4,500-foot perch on the foothills offers a dynamic view of the Wasatch Mountains to the east and the Salt Lake Valley looking west. In 2003, the state's largest sports video display system was installed in the south end zone. Behind it, on ground level, sits Olympic Cauldron Park – giving the stadium unique and historic surroundings.

Lower Left: *"Swoop" continues to be a crowd favorite.*

Lower Right: *A Ute Player fires up the crowd.*

SCOTT G. WINTERTON

TOM SMART

TOM SMART

TOM SMART

KFAN
1320 AM
FOX

Opposite: Head Coach Urban Meyer talks to the media following a practice.

Right: Meyer works the officials during Utah's win over BYU.

INNER URBAN
A Look at Coach Urban Meyer

JEFFREY D. ALLREDD

Story by LINDA HAMILTON

Once a raving maniac, Urban Meyer changed the way he coached after working for Sonny Lubick at Colorado State.

Meyer had learned his coaching at the feet of Earle Bruce, when both were at Ohio State, home of Woody Hayes. It was a hands-on style, as in coaches grabbing players by the facemask and screaming at them. Maybe worse. When the CSU player quit, Sonny Lubick called Meyer into his office for a calm-down talk. Lubick had replaced Bruce as coach of the Rams and retained the impressive young Meyer, but an alteration was in order.

"He changed the way I coached," says a grateful Meyer. Lubick coaches gently, and he set Meyer on a new path that day in 1993 in Fort Collins. "I became a better coach when I found out you could be a human being. I used to be an absolute raving maniac," said Meyer, who changed because "I just saw it work. I said, 'I might even live longer now.' "

Meyer knew he got his blood pressure out of whack with his wild style, and he had never before given himself time to jog or sleep or pay attention to life.

Billy Gonzales, who played receiver under Meyer at CSU and has been one of his assistant coaches both at Bowling Green University and at Utah, saw the change

TOM SMART

TOM SMART

JEFFREY D. ALLRED

***Top:** The Meyer Family: Urban, Gigi, Shelley, Nathan and Nicole.*

***Above:** Coach Meyer and his wife Shelley thank the crowd after a recent victory.*

first-hand. Gonzales, though, remembers that Ram receivers had a feeling Meyer would mellow as soon as his wife, Shelley, had their first child. Gonzales said that's what he saw - "When he became a father, he became a better coach."

Shelley Meyer saw the change, too. Her husband wasn't that interested in children until Nicole, now 12, came along; then he embraced the family concept. "He's a great dad," says Shelley, who nevertheless insists on a week's vacation every year to get him away from football.

He comes home at 10 p.m. and plays catch with 10-year-old Gigi, who plays shortstop on boys' Little League teams, and during this fall's training camp, he had the kids stay with him in the dorms so they could be together more. The couple of months that the family stayed in Bowling Green while he was in Utah working his new job were the hardest he's endured.

He was so miserable that linebacker Ray Holdcraft came into his office to specifically ask if the coach was all right. Meyer admits he did "a poor job" handling his players those first two months. A talk with former Jazz president/general manager/coach Frank Layden helped Meyer see the big picture. Meyer is as driven as ever. That hasn't changed. He still yells at players with the best of them, and he demands extreme conditioning and attention to both studies and the game that he dearly loves. But he may also call aside a recently-berated player for a friendly discussion and pat on the back, and he is as effusive with compliments as complaints.

It's rare for an avowed taskmaster to be compassionate, but Meyer excels at both. "He's just as intense," Gonzales observes. "Stern. But at the same time, he's a player's coach." Meyer, in fact, is the reason Gonzales got into coaching.

He's both a dynamo, who takes on too many tasks and does them all well, and a highly personable man, who really takes the time to get to know those he meets, delving into their interests, even though there isn't time for that.

"If somebody wants to speak to Urban, he'll find the time," says Meyer's best friend, Jerry Batt, a Bowling Green booster who says BGSU players still call Meyer to chat. "There's a trust factor with the man."

Batt and Meyer are similar in age, their wives are both competitive volleyball players, and their children are compatible, so the families quickly became close after Meyer took the Bowling Green job in 2001. The Batts have already visited Salt Lake City and plan to come again.

BGSU was Meyer's first head-coaching experience, one he got after assisting for five years at Notre Dame. "He got the most out of the talent he had," Batt said of Meyer's two years at Bowling Green, where he took a team that hadn't had a winning season since 1994 to a Top 20 national ranking in mid-2002. "He loves what he does."

Utah's new football coach grew up on the northeast Ohio shores of Lake Erie, in Ashtabula, the son of a chemical engineer (Urban "Bud" Meyer) and a gourmet chef (Gisela), who arrived in the United States from Bavaria in 1959 and first met Bud at a restaurant in Cincinnati.

Bud is the fourth in a family line of "only sons", his football-coach son is the fifth, and 4-year-old Nathan is the sixth to so far have no brothers. "The next one will be a warlock," predicts Bud, who uses that name to distinguish himself from his father, Urban, and his son, Urban. They were named for a pope.

The third Urban spent his youth attending Catholic schools, crewing in sailboat races on Lake Erie, trying to keep up academically with his two gifted sisters and playing sports, always under his father's watchful eye.

"He was ordinary. Nothing was unusual about him," says Bud, who instilled the urgency to excel in his children. "I lived in such a competitive household," says Meyer. He admits he's closer to his dad now than he was as a kid when he had to study videotapes of his ballgames, made by his father, to learn to play better. That was tough, but at the same time, his father made time to be at every game.

"It was a household of high achievement," Urban says. He remembers getting a "C" in English once. "I didn't think the sun would come up the next day." "I just felt I'd better do right. I got away with nothing."

Though young Urban did household chores, he got no allowance. He couldn't have a summer job or watch television. He and his sisters were encouraged instead to do things that would keep them active and stay with them - sports or music. His sisters were "brilliant", Meyer says. He wanted to play professional sports.

The way to earn money, for Urban, was to hit home runs ($1) or doubles (50 cents) or do other positive things athletic. For outs or errors, he had to pay his father.

Urban's wardrobe was thin. He had only one pair of jeans. But, "if I wanted a baseball glove, I got the best on the market," he says. He had a Wilson A2000, and so does Gigi. When Urban messed up, he had to run laps around the house and do pushups."I know Bud drove him real hard," says Shelley, adding that her husband makes his children do laps and pushups for their indiscretions, too.

Perhaps that background led Urban to the weight room far earlier than most athletes. "It used to be taboo," he recalls, but he was inspired by a magazine article about the Nebraska Cornhuskers and their weightlifting. "I lifted all the time." He slept in a sweatshirt "so I wouldn't hurt my arm." An undersized safety/running back/shortstop, he was always looking for an edge.

"Even as a little kid I thought, 'How can I outwork them?'" He went to batting cages and did all he could until a growth spurt between his sophomore and junior years took him to 6-foot-1."Line drives turned into home runs," and his football career went from "nowhere" to all-state and Division I scholarship offers.He was drafted in the 13th round by the Atlanta Braves, and a family friend who coached at Cleveland State and who had pitched in the big leagues told the Meyers that, if he could play pro ball, he should. The youngest player drafted that year at 17, he soon found that being "a great high school player doesn't necessarily make a great pro." Two years of riding buses, eating Egg McMuffins, grilled cheese sandwiches and KFC offset the thrill of hitting .300 in his second season in a high Class A league.

No longer eligible for a college scholarship as a former pro, Urban spent a year at Cleveland State and then walked onto the University of Cincinnati football team. He helped coach at various schools and didn't play football as a senior, becoming a student assistant coach instead. Still not willing to say his son is anything out of the ordinary, Bud says Urban got a graduate assistant's job with Bruce at Ohio State "on the coattails of a good quarterback" friend who went there. Shelley Mather met Meyer in May 1984 at college. She already had a boyfriend and turned Meyer down when he asked her out, but she couldn't get him out of her head for three weeks until he tried again. "I couldn't stop thinking about him. He was really cute, very funny. I couldn't say no," Shelley says, adding that, except for one day, they've been together ever since. "I wasn't a football fanatic then like I am now," she says. He was just starting to talk about becoming a coach in those days, at least to her.

Batt says Meyer has had his whole life planned out. Meyer says the idea came to him back when he was reading the weightlifting magazines, which contained pictures of great coaches that he put on his wall. His father took him to a Cincinnati-Michigan State game when he was 8 or 9; he met a defensive coach and watched him throughout the game. "Mesmerized" by the intensity and strategy he saw, that became his profession of choice.

Shelley, who became a psychiatric nurse and works as an instructor at the U., didn't know what she was getting into. When he got a job at Illinois State and wanted her to come with him, she balked. "I can't just follow my boyfriend all over the U.S.," she told her companion of four years. They soon were engaged, then married, but she never saw him as he worked 6 a.m. until midnight or later at ISU.

"I started to figure out what kind of career this was going to be. What have we gotten into?" she thought. He was feeling the same way, embarrassed by his yearly paycheck of $6,200. He was ready to quit, but Shelley wouldn't let him, and soon he got a call from Bruce to join the OSU staff. Bruce was later fired but resurfaced at Colorado State, a move Shelley very much approved. The Meyers learned to ski and loved the mountains, and the football team did reasonably well, but Bruce was fired again. With Shelley seven months pregnant, Meyer took a job at UTEP, but three weeks later, Lubick brought him back to CSU. A good Catholic could hardly turn down a coaching opportunity at Notre Dame, but Shelley, who'd had her first two children in Fort Collins and loved the mountains, hated moving back to the flatlands. When the Bowling Green job came up, she knew it was best, but all she could think of was, "No, that's the wrong way!" East, not west. "When the Utah thing came up, I said, 'Oh, yeah, yeah, yeah!'"

Though she hasn't always been happy with football coaching, she has three times kept Urban from quitting this profession, in which he's become one of the hottest names in the country. Bud Meyer's "ordinary" son, who got a 3.3 GPA in arts and sciences and did graduate work in psychology, has done well for one who's intense "from not wanting to take a lunchbox to work. He's a stickler because, if you don't do that, you're not doing your job," according to Bud. "I guess he picked up some of his (football) savvy from some of the people that taught him - Bruce, Lou Holtz, Lubick - he gave Urban another whole dimension on things, but he learned the most from Earle."

Urban credits his father for his drive and sense that whatever he does, "You'd better be good at it." And despite his rather meteoric rise - a product of intense preparation and what Gonzales calls his boss's "unbelievable" comprehension of football's X's and O's - Meyer still sweats out thoughts that he might have left some stone unturned.

"My worst fear is underachieving. That's what drives me every day," he says.

***Top:** Meyer has had some great mentors like Earle Bruce, Lou Holtz and Sonny Lubick.*

***Bottom:** Meyer possesses an unbelievable comprehension of football's X's and O's.*

JEFFREY D. ALLRED

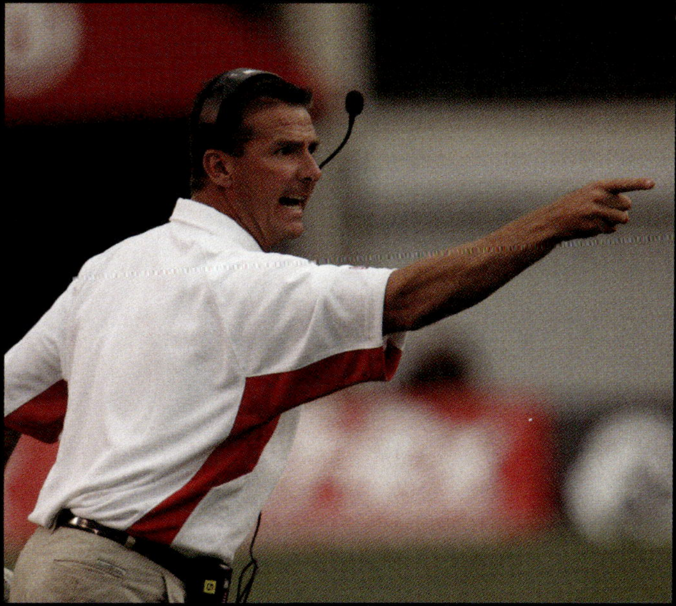

TOM SMART

UTAH FOOTBALL
Telex

COACHING STAFF
Built for Success

Opposite: *Quarterbacks coach Dan Mullen, head coach Urban Meyer and receiver coach Billy Gonzales helped Utah's offense achieve national prominence.*

Right: *Utah head coach Urban Meyer and defensive line coach Gary Andersen celebrate after a big play by the Utes.*

TOM SMART

Urban Meyer isn't surprised that defensive coordinator Kyle Whittingham and offensive coordinator Mike Sanford wound up with promotions. Each played a pivotal role in Utah's back-to-back outright league championships.

Their efforts helped the Utes finish the regular season as the Mountain West Conference's leader in numerous categories, including pass efficiency offense (171.61 rating), total offense (502.73 ypg), scoring offense (46.27 ppg) and pass efficiency defense (108.06 rating). They were second in rushing offense (244.91 ypg), passing defense (198.91 ypg), total defense (350.27 ypg) and scoring defense (20.64 ppg).

"I think when you hire coordinators, you hire people who can become head coaches. I think, without question, Kyle Whittingham is going to be a terrific head coach, and I think Mike Sanford is going to be a terrific head coach," said Meyer. "I think down the road I have other coaches on our staff that, as they move up the ranks, will be head coaches."

Whittingham, who spent 10 seasons as Utah's defensive coordinator, was Meyer's choice to take over as head coach. When athletic director Chris Hill agreed and

TOM SMART

Top Left: *Quarterbacks coach Dan Mullen gives instructions to Alex Smith.*

TOM SMART

TOM SMART

TOM SMART

ultimately convinced Whittingham to accept the job and not return to his alma mater – the Team Down South – as head coach, Meyer called it a move that will keep the Utes in the national rankings for years to come.

"I'm excited about keeping what we've got going with Urban Meyer. The discipline structure, the academics, everything he put in place I firmly believe in. But, it's not going to be Urban Meyer, part two," said Whittingham, who noted his flavor and personality will be incorporated into schemes. "The direction that we're heading right now is where we're going to stay. Expectations are high."

At a press conference announcing the hiring, Whittingham announced that defensive line coach Gary Andersen would replace him as coordinator. The former Southern Utah head coach is credited with developing tackles Sione Pouha and Steve Fifita into first-team all-conference performers.

Whittingham and Andersen are close friends and the transition promises to be smooth. The duo, along with linebackers coach Kurt Barber and cornerbacks coach Chuck Heater, helped direct a 2004 defense that complimented a high-powered offense.

With Sanford calling the plays, the Utes ranked among the nation's top nine offenses in four major statistical categories – rushing, pass efficiency, total yardage and point production.

The numbers helped propel quarterback Alex Smith into the national spotlight. The Heisman Trophy finalist was named player of the year by *The Sporting News and Sports Illustrated.*

Such success proved costly, however.

Shortly after the regular season came to an end, Sanford was hired to replace the retiring John Robinson as head coach at league foe UNLV.

"Mike Sanford has an excellent offensive mind. He has been a big part of our success this year," said Meyer. "He is not only a great coach, but a great person. Mike will do an outstanding job at UNLV."

After the Fiesta Bowl, quarterback coach Dan Mullen, receiver coach Billy Gonzales and offensive line coach Dan Hevesy ended two-year tenures at Utah by opting to join Meyer in Florida. Tight ends coach Keith Uperesa will join Sanford in Las Vegas.

Oregon's Andy Ludwig was hired as a Utah's new offensive coordinator. He inherits a scheme that scored more points than any team in Utah history.

SCOTT G. WINTERTON

TOM SMART

Middle Left: *Defensive coordinator Kyle Whittingham in an intense moment.*

Bottom Left: *Offensive line coach John Hevesy and quarterbacks coach Dan Mullen don headsets during a game.*

Bottom Middle: *Kyle Whittingham will move from defensive coordinator to head coach next season.*

Bottom Right: *Defensive line coach Gary Andersen will become the team's defensive coordinator in 2005.*

UTAH UTES

ALEX SMITH
As Good As It Gets

Opposite: Utah quarterback Alex Smith struggles to keep his weight up despite a steady diet of pizzas.

Right: Alex Smith developed into Utah's first Heisman Trophy finalist while leading the Utes to a berth in the Bowl Championship Series. He was named player of the year by The Sporting News and Sports Illustrated.

TOM SMART

Story by MIKE SORENSEN

At the time, Alex Smith was pretty upset at then-coach Ron McBride for costing him a year of eligibility. As a freshman quarterback in 2002, Smith was used for just a handful of plays during a desperate period of McBride's final season at Utah.

He was inserted into a losing game at San Diego State for a few plays, only to have a pass intercepted for a touchdown. After that, he only threw one more pass, two weeks later in an overtime loss to New Mexico. It seemed like such a waste of a redshirt season at the time. But now Smith wonders what he would do if he had to attend three years of graduate school while completing his football eligibility. "I don't know what I would have done," Smith said. "It turned out well." Plus, the way Smith played football this season, there's probably no way he could stick around for two more years, and there's speculation he may not return for his senior season because of his unexpected success. In just two seasons, Smith has become one of the nation's top quarterbacks. This year he has collected several honors, including *Sports Illustrated* Player of the Year, *Sporting News Player of the Year,* second-team A.P. all-American, and Mountain West Conference Player of the Year. He was also invited to the Heisman Trophy Award Ceremony in New York after finishing fourth in the nationwide balloting. Since becoming the Ute starter almost by default when starter Brett Elliott went down with an injury, Smith has won 20 of his 21 starts and led the Utes to an undefeated season this year. Smith has led the Utes to 15 straight victories, including 11 straight this season, heading into the Fiesta Bowl. Not only has Smith excelled on the football field, he also excels in the class-

Jeffrey D. Allred

Below: *Alex Smith worked his way onto the national scene as a junior. The durable quarterback has played in every game since replacing the injured Brett Elliott early in the 2003 season.*

Jeffrey D. Allred

room. Smith earned first-team academic all-American honors. He is the quintessential "student-athlete,'' as the NCAA loves to refer to collegiate athletes, whether the student part fits or not. In Smith's case, the title more than applies.

The son of a high school principal, Smith has always taken his studies seriously. In high school he was an A student and he took every A.P. (advanced placement) test he could. Of the 14 tests he took, he passed 12, which helped knock two years off his college requirements. When he arrived at Utah, he discovered he had 64 hours of credit, putting him more than halfway to graduation. Being an excellent student already, it wasn't hard for Smith to complete his bachelor's degree during his first two years, compiling a 3.79 GPA. That makes him unusual among his teammates, most of whom are doing their best to complete their undergraduate degree in four or five years. Even the handful who already have their degrees are seniors, not juniors like Smith. "It's different for me because I'm so far ahead," said Smith, who is working toward a master's degree in economics in the U.'s two-year program. At least he's not feeling overburdened as a graduate student. "I have kind of a light semester, which is nice because I can concentrate on football,'' he said. Smith still has the minimum of 12 hours. But along with three economics classes, he has three PE classes, including a bowling class (let's hope he doesn't injure that precious right arm at the alley). Smith plans to make up for his light schedule, saying, "I can load up in spring and summer.''

Jeffrey D. Allred

It's probably fortunate that Smith had a lighter than usual load this fall. As the Utes keep winning and Smith keeps playing so well, the requests for interviews have kept growing. Utah sports information director Liz Abel has been busy all fall trying to accommodate the many requests for Smith. Besides the daily interviews with the local media, he does about a dozen interviews with out-of-state media every week. Already this season he's talked to reporters from *ESPN News, USA Today, the New York Times, Chicago Tribune, Denver Post, L.A. Times, ESPN Magazine, and Sports Illustrated* and has appeared on shows such as ESPN's "Cold Pizza" morning show. It might be a bit mind-boggling or at least distracting for a 20-year-old, but Smith handles it with aplomb, patiently answering every question and making sure each reporter gets all that he needs before moving along to the next. "He's been great,'' said Abel. "He doesn't complain and spends all the time (the media) needs.'' He became so popular that over the last month of the season, Smith needed to cut his interview schedule to Monday and Wednesday afternoons. Smith's smarts have certainly helped him on the football field. He's a good but not great runner and has an adequate, though not especially strong arm. But it's his ability to pick apart defenses and his penchant for always making the correct decision that sets Smith apart from other quarterbacks. No wonder Smith has earned so many awards this season. The big question is whether or not Smith will be back for his senior season. He said he'd like to play another year, but if he's projected to go in the first two rounds, he'll likely put his name into the NFL draft. If and when Smith finishes his master's degree, he'd like to attend law school, though not necessarily to be a lawyer. "I'd like to get my J.D. degree because it opens a lot of doors,'' he said. "It's something I've always wanted to do.'' Utah fans hope he returns for his senior season but would understand if he can earn big bucks by turning pro. "He's gone from being a third-string quarterback to the best in college football,'' said Utah coach Urban Meyer. "I know some other guys have put up great numbers, but I still believe Alex is as good as anybody in the country.''

Left: *Running back Quinton Ganther provides quarterback Alex Smith some assistance in the weight room.*

PAGE 95
The many faces of Utah quarterback Alex Smith -- graduate student, football fanatic and the pride of Salt Lake City.

Jeffrey D. Allred

Jeffrey D. Allred

Jeffrey D. Allred

Scott G. Winterton

MARTY JOHNSON
Against All Odds

Opposite: Once-troubled running back Marty Johnson returned to the Utes as a changed man after overcoming a pair of DUIs and a lengthy team suspension.

Right: Utah coach Urban Meyer took a chance on running back Marty Johnson and it paid off handsomely for the Utes.

JEFFREY D. ALLRED

Story by MIKE SORENSEN

Perhaps the tattoo on Marty Johnson's left forearm - "Against All Odds" - said it best.

After battling two season-ending injuries, being arrested twice for DUIs, serving 30 miserable days in jail, undergoing treatment for alcohol abuse and adhering to stringent guidelines set by his coaches for nearly a year, Johnson came back to the Utah football team in 2004 and became a big factor in the Utes' unbeaten season. The 6-foot, 225-pound running back had shown glimpses of greatness in three games he played for Utah during the 2001 and 2002 seasons that ended with injuries. After all his setbacks, he rejoined the Utes for the 2004 season, staying healthy the entire year and starting nearly every game. Johnson led the Utes in rushing with 782 yards, scored 14 touchdowns and also caught six passes out of the backfield. He didn't exhibit the breakaway speed he had a couple of years earlier, but was a reliable performer in the Ute offense, counted on especially in short-yardage situations. When confronted with his past problems, whether by local reporters or the national media, Johnson didn't run away. He would patiently answer every question and pull no punches while talking about all the lows he went through over the previous two years. He talked about the frustration of his injuries, his problems with alcohol, the treat-

TOM SMART

ment he went through (which he had to pay for himself) how he was hanging out with a whole new group of friends, and how he changed his overall lifestyle.

Johnson's problems began soon after the knee injury in the Indiana game in 2002, which happened a year after a rib injury knocked him out after the Utah State game. He was leading the nation in rushing at the time, with over 400 yards in two games. However, without football in his life, he got into trouble when he drove his vehicle into a parked car. He was convicted of a class B misdemeanor DUI and a class B misdemeanor for leaving the scene of the accident. After the season, Meyer took over for Ron McBride and the new coach gave Johnson a chance to redeem himself. But last September, Johnson crashed his car over a curb and was arrested with his blood alcohol level more than twice the legal limit. He was sentenced to 30 days in jail, two years probation, 120 hours of community service and fined $1,500. He also was ordered to continue alcohol treatment, which he had to pay for out of his own pocket. At that point, Meyer could have given up on Johnson, but instead went out of his way to help him overcome his alcohol problems and get his life in order. "Coach Meyer helped me realize it was a problem and that I should take care of it,'' said Johnson. "I really didn't think it was a problem until I started looking at myself.'' Meyer said he didn't want to turn his back on the young man. "I've done this for 19 years and dealt with more than 2,000 football players over the years and I don't know if I've ever seen anybody reach the bottom as far as he did,'' said Meyer. "He had depression, no desire to compete and really had to crawl out of a hole." What really opened Johnson's eyes was the month he had to spend in jail. "There were some nice people in there, but even they talked to me and said that wasn't where I should be,'' he said. "The judge said if I got in any more trouble, I'd go back for a year and I couldn't imagine doing it for a year.

That month was hard. Johnson was not allowed to be part of the team and had to fulfill several requirements to get back on the team, including finishing his degree in sociology, staying clean from alcohol and staying out of any trouble. "I was willing to do anything it would take,'' said Johnson. "I wanted to play football so bad.'' Last March, before spring practice began, Meyer said he wasn't concerned about Johnson's ability on the field. "I'm worried about him not being a guy who is a menace to society and if he is going to be a guy who will do the right thing. I think there is some good in that person and if we can pull the good out then we've done our job,'' Meyer said at the time. But Meyer is pleased with the progress Johnson has made. "He's been great,'' Meyer said. "He has his degree and he's doing what he loves to do, which is play football. He's living his life for the first time the way he's supposed to live it.'' Instead of partying, Johnson started watching movies with his girlfriend, and playing video games or cards, or "hanging out" with guys such as Alex Smith, Morgan Scalley, Eric Weddle and Bryan Borreson. "At first I was like, 'What am I doing hanging out with the kicker (Borreson)," Johnson said with a laugh. "But I started having fun, playing cards and stuff.'' Johnson was so excited about playing for the first time in two years, he would wake up at 4 or 5 in the morning, thinking about the upcoming games. He began practicing with the team during spring drills, but wasn't officially on the team until the start of fall practice. Being away from the game for two years gave Johnson a new appreciation for practice. "It's been so fun to be back with my teammates, I've even started to like practice,'' he said early in the season. In his first game back, he gained 77 yards against Texas A&M and in the fourth game he scored four touchdowns in the win over Air Force. The next game he picked up 99 yards in a road win over New Mexico and had his best yardage game with 105 yards in the late-season win at Wyoming. After his problems with alcohol, Johnson says he's physically in the best shape of his life this season and that his "body feels great." He's grateful for the opportunity coach Meyer gave him and the support of his teammates. "He's obviously changed his lifestyle,'' said Smith. "He's worked really hard to get where he is. I can't say enough for him how hard he's worked.''

MITCH DUMKE

Senior tailback Marty Johnson wound up leading the Utes in rushing in his first full season with the team.

Utah's leading receivers in 2004 (from left to right): John Madsen, Travis LaTendresse, Steve Savoy and Paris Warren.

WIDE RECEIVERS

Perfect Reception

AUGUST MILLER

Utah's receivers have been under scrutiny throughout the Urban Meyer era. The coach's spread offense, he notes, requires depth and experience at the position.

After Meyer's first spring with the Utes, he didn't hedge his thoughts on the topic. "Without question, receiver is the biggest concern on our team," Meyer said in the team's 2003 media guide. "When we first arrived at Utah we felt we were inadequate at receiver," he recalled.

Led by Oregon transfer Paris Warren, who earned first-team All-Mountain West Conference recognition after hauling in a school-record 76 receptions, many of Meyer's concerns were alleviated that season. The development of Steve Savoy, Travis LaTendresse and John Madsen provided quarterback Alex Smith with some solid targets. "Receiver has gone from a weakness to one of our anticipated strengths," Meyer said in the 2004 preview.

The prediction proved accurate.

Utah followed a 10-2 season with an 11-0 campaign. Smith completed 185-of-280 passes for 2,624 yards en route to finishing fourth in the Heisman Trophy balloting. He was intercepted just four times while throwing for 28 scores – all but two were caught by either Warren, Savoy, LaTendresse or Madsen.

Bottom Right: *Senior captain Paris Warren*

Below Top to Bottom: *Sophomore Steve Savoy, Senior Travis LaTendresse, and Junior John Madsen.*

AUGUST MILLER

AUGUST MILLER

AUGUST MILLER

"They're huge. When we got out to Utah there wasn't a whole lot of experience," said quarterback coach Dan Mullen. "One of the reasons for Alex's success this year is that all those guys came back with that experience."

Utah's top four receivers each upped their yardage this season. Savoy had the biggest increase -- going from 663 receiving yards to a team-high 891. Warren went from 809 to 878, while LaTendresse improved to 402 from 366. Madsen increased his contributions by 20 catches as his receiving yardage swelled to 350 from 97.

"If you have one good receiver you can eliminate him. If you have two good receivers you can almost eliminate them," said Meyer. "But, if you have three or four, you can't."

The foursome combined to catch 27 touchdown passes (Madsen teamed with back-up quarterback Brian Johnson for a score). Savoy, a first-team all-conference honoree, topped the team with 11. Warren, a second-team selection, had 10. Madsen and LaTendresse scored four and two times, respectively.

"In this offense the good guys catch it. Guys that aren't so good are decoys and there's ways to do that," said Meyer. "Those four guys are all very good receivers."

Each brings something different to Utah's high-powered offense. Smith, who was named national player of the year by *The Sporting News, and Sports Illustrated* said it's a tribute to those around him. The Utes have been especially good at throwing the ball. Smith had the second-best pass efficiency rating (174.9) in the country.

"I think the neat thing about our offense is you can move people around to get them the ball. You do play four receivers most times, sometimes five receivers," said Meyer. "The defense still has to cover them and so the good thing about Travis, John Madsen, Savoy and Paris is they're all interchangeable and you can move them around to where you want to get them. Maybe we don't have the depth, but it seemed like we did because we always had good guys catch the ball," added Meyer.

One, however, has stood above the others. Warren, Meyer said, may have the made the team's greatest contributions on offense. The senior captain's performances, he continued, rival or surpass those of Smith and offensive center Jesse Boone.

"If you had to say who the Most Valuable Player on offense was I would say it's Paris Warren," said Meyer. "Paris Warren did a lot of things. His savvy and command of the offense is the best I've ever seen a receiver have."

Savoy, a sophomore, has shown the potential to do the same.

"Paris is a complete receiver and Steve showed signs this year," said Meyer, who noted that Savoy had a bad outing against Arizona. He scored two touchdowns in the game, but failed to please the coaching staff in terms of blocking, missed assignments and effort. The shortcomings were addressed and Meyer praised Savoy for working with receivers coach Billy Gonzales to become one of the team's better blockers. Savoy's athleticism make him extremely versatile. He scored six touchdowns rushing, including a 92-yard romp in the season-ending 52-21 win over BYU.

"Steve Savoy is not the complete guy yet," said Meyer. "But if he keeps going he could become that."

Consistent improvement has transformed Madsen into a threat. He didn't play high school football, but has gradually made up for it. The 6-foot-5 former basketball player, Meyer explained, no longer looks like a guy who hasn't played much football. He's just kept improving and improving.

"I think he's going to play in the NFL, I really do. You can't teach size and speed and he's got them both," said Meyer. "He's a great kid and a great worker."

LaTendresse also has a strong work ethic. The seven-time Junior Olympic gold medalist in Tae Kwon Do brings an enhanced element of toughness to Utah's receiving corps.

"Although he was dinged up most of the year. He was also a valuable guy," said Meyer. "He made some great catches. The perfect example is the one down the middle against BYU, where he separated his shoulder. How many guys on your team do that -- take a hit like that and still hold onto the ball?"

Such contributions, Meyer explained, are commonplace with Utah's top receivers.

"I think those four guys, as a team, are as good as any receivers certainly in the Mountain West Conference," said Meyer. "And a lot of other places as well."

AUGUST MILLER

Senior captain Morgan Scalley gets a lift from teammate Spencer Toone.

MORGAN SCALLEY

Born To Be A Ute

TOM SMART

Story by MIKE SORENSEN

When he was a little kid, Morgan Scalley thought his dad was a big football star. He remembers admiring his trophies, including one that sort of resembled the famous Heisman Trophy.

Of course Bud Scalley never won the Heisman when he played for the University of Utah more than 40 years ago. He did receive a scholarship trophy as a senior and the trophy little Morgan thought was the Heisman was actually one that Bud received from coaching Morgan's older brother in Mighty Mites football. The fact is, in his whole collegiate career at Utah, Bud Scalley only gained about the same number of yards as a Heisman winner today might get in a single game. But he was a feisty competitor who will always be remembered by Ute old-timers for one moment of glory, when he scored the winning, and only, touchdown in an unforgettable victory over a nationally-ranked, unbeaten, Merlin Olsen-led Utah State team in 1960.

The 1960 media guide lists Bud Scalley as one of the 60 players on the Utah football team, although he didn't warrant a number on the roster. The preseason four-deep chart didn't even list Scalley, a 19-year-old sophomore, as one of the top 12 backs (two halfbacks and a fullback) on the team. Scalley played for Bear River High School and walked on the U. team as a freshman, back when freshmen weren't eligible and there was a separate freshman team. After a good spring game that sea-

Morgan Scalley scored two touchdowns this season - one on a fumble recovery and the other on a kickoff return. The Utah senior earned All-America honors as a safety.

son, Scalley was invited to play for the varsity. By the time the season started, the 5-9, 162-pound Scalley had worked his way up to fourth string. By midseason he was third string. He made an impression on the Utah coaches in a November game at Colorado State, for a couple of mistakes he made, including one that turned out to be a touchdown for the Utes. While fielding a punt during the pre-game warm-ups, Scalley inadvertently ran into a table on the sidelines where the scoreboard operation was set up, collapsing it and delaying the start of the game. One of the Utah assistant coaches was so impressed, he told the team, "I want you guys concentrating like Scalley today." Later in the game Utah coach Ray Nagel called for Stanley Uyeshiro, the team's leading rusher that season, to go in at halfback. Scalley thought Nagel said "Scalley" instead of "Stanley" and ran into the game, where he promptly scored a touchdown. It wasn't until the bus ride back to Denver that Nagel told Scalley about the miscommunication. Two weeks later, on November 19, Ute Stadium was packed with the third largest crowd in history. The Utes were 6-2 and going up against a 9-0 Aggie team featuring Merlin Olsen and ranked No. 16 in the nation. The game was a defensive battle, as the Utah defense shut down the Aggies' great runner, Tom Larscheid. During the game, the Utes' top two halfbacks, Jerry Overton and Dennis Zito, were both sidelined, Overton with a broken leg and Zito with a knee injury. That left Scalley, who was up to the challenge. "They had no one else to use," he said, "so I played the remainder of the game." With 6:15 left, Scalley, as reported in the Deseret News, "skirted the left side for 12 yards and the winning touchdown." "They said it couldn't be done, but we did it," Scalley said, smiling at the memory of the unforgettable 6-0 victory 44 years ago.

TOM SMART

Sitting in his parents east-side condominium one recent afternoon, Morgan Scalley laughs at the memory. "I grew up thinking he was the Heisman Trophy winner," he said. Even when he discovered his father wasn't the best player in America and only rushed for 337 yards in his career, Morgan still wanted to be like his dad and become a running back for Utah. "That was my dream, that's what I wanted to do, follow in my dad's footsteps," he said. "I knew he wasn't the biggest player out there. But I grew up loving the game and knowing how it should be played because of him." Bud gave his son a good start in football, coaching him beginning at age eight up until junior high school. Morgan still remembers his first practice, with players doing a one-on-one drill. He was eyeing the opposite line, relieved to see a kid about his size matched up against him. However, when it came time to hit the opposing player, his dad grabbed a large Polynesian kid out of the line to go against Morgan. After literally getting the snot knocked out of him, Morgan pulled himself up off the turf and said to himself, "He's not going to cut me any slack." Bud, who had been a boxer growing up in northern Utah, had become a college football player largely because of his toughness, and he was going to make sure his son had the same quality. Morgan also had speed and quickness, something Bud claims he never had, which helped him score numerous touchdowns in little league and in high school. He also was imbued with the family's competitive spirit ("If you saw one of our family Rook games, someone was always walking away crying or throwing the cards down," Morgan said). As a sophomore at Highland High School, Scalley was only about 5-foot-5, 125 pounds, not exactly the size you want to be to play football. One day when he told his mother, Claudia, of his dream to play college football, she sighed and diplomatically told him, 'Don't feel hurt if it doesn't happen." "Frankly, we didn't think he'd go that far," Bud said. By the time the playoffs came around that sophomore year, Scalley was returning kickoffs for the Rams. The next year he was a backup running back, but when the starter went down in the pre-game warm-ups before the first game, Scalley was moved up and held the position for the next two seasons. After an all-state senior season, Scalley had interest from schools such as UCLA, Washington State, Air Force and BYU. He didn't take any out-of-state visits, but did take an official visit to BYU, during, of all things, the Utah-BYU game. "I stood on the Utah sideline the whole game," recalls Scalley, smiling at the memory. He committed to Utah and coach Ron McBride soon after that and later BYU assistant Norm Chow told Morgan he wished he had waited and given BYU a chance. Scalley was a "grayshirt" right out of high school, meaning he didn't attend school that first quarter. He went on a mission to Munich, Germany and returned home wondering if football was in his future. "I couldn't lift a weight to save my life,'' Morgan said. "I used to go and lift at Highland because I was too embarrassed to lift at the U. My legs didn't come back until the end of my freshman season." Nevertheless, Scalley played that first season back in 2001 and was used as the Utes' primary punt returner, returning 26 kicks for 249 yards. "It scared me to death,'' he said. "There was so much pressure. It was a tough first year.'' He still wanted to be a running back and he was tried briefly as a receiver, but he could tell the offensive coaches at the time didn't see a future for him. However, defensive coordinator Kyle Whittingham and defensive backs coach Bill Busch were anxious to use Scalley and lobbied to get him over to the defense. But Scalley resisted. "I had always dreamed of following my dad as a running back,'' he said. "Then I slapped myself in the face one day and said, 'You idiot. You finally have coaches who want you.' I figured it was better to play for someone who wants you than have no shot with someone who doesn't want you.'' The following year, he returned punts again and was the backup safety behind Antoine Sanders. He also was the Utes' punter for the Colorado State game when the Utes employed an unusual "rugby punt" scheme with Scalley having the option of running the ball or punting on the run like he did as a high school rugby player. When Urban Meyer arrived the following season his first thought about Scalley was one of puzzlement. "I couldn't imagine why he hadn't played much,'' he said. Scalley became the starting free safety and one of Meyer's favorite players, starting all 12 games and earning second-team all-MWC honors. "He's not a good football player, he's a great football player,'' Meyer said. When the Utes were down to one running back late last season, Meyer said he considered moving Scalley over, but decided against it. "In real life, our defense is fairly complicated and it's not one of those things where you say go practice offense for awhile,'' Meyer said. "It would have been unfair to him because he's one of the best safeties in college football. But he could be a great running back and I know he could be a receiver tomorrow.''

For a kid whose own parents wondered if he had a chance to play in college, the next step may be pro football for Morgan Scalley. He still fondly remembers a trip with his dad to see a Kansas City Chiefs game as a youngster when he watched Joe Montana and met Marcus Allen. Scalley's dream is to be playing football on Sundays in the future. "I would love to, but I know scouts aren't looking for 5-10, 195-pound safeties,'' he said. "Hopefully my quickness and competitive nature will help me out.'' Because he has already earned his undergraduate degree (he was an academic all-American last year with a 3.953 GPA), Scalley is working on his MBA in finance. He's been on the student-athlete advisory committee for two years and is interested in working in athletic administration someday, perhaps as an athletic director. He still has nine games left, hopefully 10, this season and even though he was never able to walk exactly in his father's footsteps, he's grateful for his example. "I know he never won the Heisman. But to find out he was a walk-on who earned a scholarship . . . that made me think even more of him and his character.'' For his part, Bud is almost embarrassed to be mentioned in the same story as his son. "I was basically nothing more than a blocking back in college,'' he said. "He's so far ahead of anything I ever did."

JASON OLSON

Top Left: *Morgan Scalley followed in his father Bud's footsteps as a University of Utah football player.*

Right: *Eric Weddle and Morgan Scalley teamed to give the Utes the top safety duo in the Mountain West Conference, if not the nation.*

TOM SMART

OFFENSIVE LINE

Front Line Accountability

Senior offensive guard Chris Kemoeatu became an All-American in 2004.

TOM SMART

While more glamorous teammates scored touchdowns, Jesse Boone, Chris Kemoeatu, David Dirkmaat, Tavo Tupola, Makai Aalona and Eric Pettit got down-and-dirty in the trenches.

Even so, Utah's offensive linemen took ownership of point production. It's a philosophy they've adopted in becoming what head coach Urban Meyer refers to as the most improved aspect of this year's team.

"If we do what we're supposed to do, we'll score points," said offensive line coach John Hevesy. "They've bought into it."

The front-line forces helped the Utes shatter a 74-year-old school scoring record. They became just the second team in program history to average more than 40 points per game. Quarterback Alex Smith cites maturity for Utah's improvement on offense. Cohesiveness and having the entire offensive line under one coach are other reasons, he said, why things were much better up front. Increased familiarity with Meyer's spread offense is another factor.

"Last year's offensive line took a little bit of the brunt and it was just because it was the first year and there were a lot of first-year players," said Meyer, who credits

eading the charge for Utah's offense: line-men #78 Tavo Tupola, #75 Eric Pettit, #70 akai Aalona, #74 David Dirkmaat and #79 esse Boone.

TOM SMART

TOM SMART

TOM SMART

Boone for bringing the players together. "The center is always the apex of the offense, and he's doing a brilliant job with it."

Meyer is particularly impressed with Boone's leadership. It's helped strengthen the entire line. Aalona, he continued, is a prime example. Meyer said the right tackle went from "marginally adequate" to being the most improved player on the team.

"They've really taken it upon themselves to learn the offense," said Hevesy. "They understand the offense - where the ball's going and what's asked of them."

Stability up front was also a factor. Boone, Aalona, Dirkmaat, Tupola and Kemoeatu saw most of the action, while Pettit made three starts in reserve.

All of the guys, Hevesy explained, were on the same page – kind of like an expanded partnership. "They know how each other blocks, how each other makes calls and how they work," said Hevesy. "It's a hundred times easier than when you rotate different guys through."

Meyer was pleased with the line's progression under Hevesy. They formed a tight-knit group.

"You basically just learn to trust each other," said Dirkmaat. "It makes it a lot easier. You just go out there, relax and play the game."

Getting a feel for each other, added Kemoeatu, has accelerated the offensive line's improvement. They gauge their success by keeping a watchful eye over Smith. "He's the leader of our offense," said Kemoeatu, who earned All-American accolades. "We all feed off of him."

Protecting No. 11, Boone noted, "is our biggest thing." With adequate time to manuever, Smith and the Utes overpowered opponents.

Complete satisfaction, however, was never achieved. Perfection is the pinnacle.

"There's always room for improvement. (Smith) should never be touched at all or even pressured. If we work harder it'll give him the safety and security he needs," said Dirkmaat. "No one likes seeing that guy on the ground. That's the worst feeling in the world because if he goes down and gets hurt, it's on us."

Accountability is a big deal to those who work in the trenches.

TOM SMART

TOM SMART

DEFENSIVE LINE

First Line of Defense

Below: Defensive end Jonathan Fanene returned a interception 76 yards for a touchdown in Utah's 48-6 win at Utah State.

TOM SMART

Utah defensive coordinator Kyle Whittingham doesn't mince any words when it comes to starting first line of defense Steve Fifita and Sione Pouha.

"They're the best tackles in the Mountain West Conference," he said. "We have not lost the line of scrimmage in any of our games. With those two guys, coupled with Jon Fanene, we expect to win the line of scrimmage every single week. That's just a given for us."

Fifita and Pouha had career years in leading the Utes to their second consecutive outright league title. They were rewarded with first-team all-conference status.

"I think they could be as good as anybody in the country," said Utah coach Urban Meyer, who strongly encouraged the pair to reach their potential this season. "I love those two kids. They're great leaders. They're great players."

Fifita, a 6-foot, 311-pound junior, was Utah's leading tackler on the line. He scored two touchdowns – one on a 6-yard interception return and the other one on offense.

Senior captain Sione Pouha was a first-team all-conference defensive tackle for the Utes in 2004.

MITCH DUMKE

Pouha, a 6-foot-3, 330-pound senior captain, recorded his first career interception during the season. He was such a force up front that Utah's rushing defense surrendered 112 more yards per game in the three games he was sidelined with an injury.

The strong duo, who can each squat 630 pounds and are nearly able to bench press 500 pounds, take game preparation seriously. They spend a considerable amount of time in the film room.

Pouha credits much of their improvement to a better understanding of the defense.

"We know what our roles are. I think we're so comfortable with the schemes we can make our own adjustments and still know that we won't be able to hurt the scheme," said Pouha. "We can make those adjustments on the field that can kind of help us."

The return of defensive line coach Gary Andersen also proved to be a great benefit.

"Coach A. helped a lot when he came back with our technique," said Fifita. "Last year, we started getting lazy towards the end of the year, but he won't let us slip on any of our techniques or anything."

Andersen, who rejoined the Ute staff in January after a one-year stint as head coach at Southern Utah, said Pouha and Fifita were a little bit rusty. All they needed, he added, was a little fine-tuning.

"I was fortunate to have them since they were puppies when they first walked in here. Development with our technique takes a long time to be able to do it exactly how we want to do it," said Andersen. "It kind of goes in stages. When I left here a year and a half ago, I felt like those kids were about ready to kind of explode. They knew the basics."

Now, they're taking things to a new level.

"They're definitely the best tandem in the Mountain West, and I know there's some good players out there, obviously, in this conference," said Andersen. "Those two kids, when you line them up together, they're very, very impressive. They've worked hard."

Utah's defensive ends also made stellar contributions. Marquess Ledbetter, a junior, led the Utes in tackles-for-loss, while senior Jonathan Fanene had a 76-yard interception return for a touchdown in the lopsided win over Utah State.

MITCH DUMKE

TOM SMART

***Top Right:** Marquess Ledbetter was a key contributor at defensive end.*
***Bottom Right:** Nose guard Steve Fifita was one of two Utah defensive linemen to earn first-team all-league recognition.*

HEISMAN
TROPHY
PRESENTED BY
SUZUKI
THE HEISMAN
NIKE
Sean
19
MEMORIAL TROPHY

AWARDS SECTION
Honors All Around

Opposite: 2004 Heisman Trophy finalists: USC quarterback Matt Leinhart, Utah quarterback Alex Smith, USC running back Reggie Bush and Oklahoma teammates– quarterback Jason White and running back Adrian Peterson.

Right: 2004 Heisman Trophy finalist Alex Smith speaks with the media at the New York Hilton.

PHOTO COURTESY OF HEISMAN TROPHY TRUST

A big deal became even bigger when Alex Smith arrived in New York City for the Heisman Trophy presentation. *The Sporting News* had already chosen him as Player of the Year. That's when reality set in.

After watching the ceremony on television throughout his childhood, the Utah quarterback found himself on the other side of the lens. "I was like a little kid up there," Smith said. "It was so much fun." Though Smith finished fourth in the balloting – behind winner Matt Leinart of Southern Cal, as well as Oklahoma teammates Adrian Peterson and Jason White – he couldn't stop smiling. The experience, he explained, was pretty special. From riding around in limos to sitting in on the Heisman Trophy television set, Smith was truly just happy to be there. Rubbing shoulders with past winners and what he called the "who's who of college football" was just icing on the cake. By the time Smith left the New York Hilton ballroom December 11, history was made. He had sur-

PHOTO COURTESY OF HEISMAN TROPHY TRUST

Top Right: *All-American offensive lineman Chris Kemoeatu.*

Bottom Right: *Paris Warren was named second team All-Mountain West Conference in 2004.*

Below: *Morgan Scalley was named co-Defensive Player of the Year in the Mountain West Conference, as well as being named an Academic All-American by CoSIDA.*

TOM SMART

AUGUST MILLER

TOM SMART

ɔassed Lee Grosscup, who was 10th in 1957, as Utah's top Heisman finisher. In addition, Smith and fifth-place honoree Reggie Bush of USC became the first high school teammates to be finalists for the award. ESPN reported that the area surrounding Helix High near San Diego featured banners and signs congratulating the players. "It's all pretty crazy," Smith said of being a Heisman finalist. "It just speaks to the team I'm on. You look up there and not one of us has a loss. I probably wouldn't be up there if my team had lost a game. So this is all due to them." Smith voiced similar praise earlier in the week when he was named Player of the Year by *The Sporting News*. "(It's) a huge honor," said Smith. "It's a tribute to the people around me." Smith, who threw 28 touchdown passes and ran for 10 scores while leading the Utes into the Bowl Championship Series, hauled in a lot of other hardware as well. In addition to being named the CoSIDA Football Academic All-American of the Year, Smith was honored as one of the nation's elite by Cingular Wireless/ABC Sports, SI.com and the Associated Press. He was also a finalist for the Davey O'Brien and Walter Camp awards.

Several of Smith's teammates also earned recognition for their roles in Utah's first 11-0 regular season. Offensive lineman Chris Kemoeatu was named an All-American by AP, SI.com and Cingular Wireless/ABC Sports. Safety Morgan Scalley was bestowed by AP, SI.com and the CoSIDA Academic All-American team. Wide receiver Steve Savoy netted honors from SI.com and *The Sporting News*, while cornerback Ryan Smith garnered second-team freshman All-American status from *TSN*. Urban Meyer also got into the act. Before earning national coach of the year honors, he picked up his second consecutive Mountain West Conference coaching accolade.

"This is not about me," he said. "I won this award because our players played extremely hard for us." Guiding the fifth-ranked Utes to back-to-back outright league titles, Meyer explained, took a team effort. An accomplishment made possible by various contributions. "I think the beauty of the thing is the players know that," said Meyer. "I wish there was a way to give away (coordinator and position coaches of the year) awards. I would certainly do that." Meyer joins mentor Sonny Lubick of Colorado State (1999, 2000) as the league's only two-time and consecutive coach of the year honorees.

Utah claimed two other individual honors when the MWC released its all-conference teams for 2004. Smith became the first Ute to win the league's Offensive Player of the Year honors. Scalley garnered co-Defensive Player of the Year recognition with San Diego State linebacker Kirk Morrison. Scalley was the first Utah defender to claim that award since John Frank in 1999. Smith, a Heisman Trophy candidate and a finalist for the Davey O'Brien Award, is 20-1 as Utah's starting quarterback. The junior led the league in total offense (289.7 ypg), passing (238.5 ypg), pass efficiency (174.9 rating) and points responsible (20.73 ppg). "Urban Meyer

First team All-Mountain West Conference receiver Steve Savoy

TOM SMART

***Top Left:** First team All-Mountain West Conference defensive lineman Sione Pouha.*

***Bottom Left:** Honorable mention All-Mountain West Conference running back Quinton Ganther.*

***Top Right:** Ryan Smith was named to the second team of The Sporting News Freshman All-American squad.*

***Bottom Right:** Defensive lineman Steve Fifita was named first team All-Mountain West Conference in 2004.*

MITCH DUMKE

TOM SMART

TOM SMART

TOM SMART

without Alex Smith is not conference coach of the year. I've made the comment that Alex Smith is the best quarterback in college football," Meyer said. "Morgan Scalley might be the top safety in college football. I don't know because I haven't studied them as close, but certainly his play and his leadership make him as valuable of a player as I've ever seen on a team." Scalley intercepted six passes in seven league games. He scored two touchdowns this season - on a 90-yard kickoff return and on a school-record 88-yard fumble recovery.

Scalley and Smith were among six Utes (tying New Mexico for league-high honors) named to the All-MWC first team. Savoy, Kemoeatu, nose guard Steve Fifita and defensive tackle Sione Pouha were the others. Wide receiver Paris Warren, tailback Marty Johnson, center Jesse Boone and safety Eric Weddle were second-team selections, while offensive lineman Makai Aalona, running back Quinton Ganther, middle linebacker Tommy Hackenbruck, punter Matt Kovacevich and outside linebacker Spencer Toone made honorable mention. Meyer was surprised Warren, Toone and Weddle weren't first-team selections. They had every intangible needed, he said, including statistics and the fact that Utah finished on top. "There's never a politically correct way to do it because everybody feels strongly about their players," said Meyer.

TOM SMART

Top Left: *Second team All-Mountain West Conference running back Marty Johnson.*

Top Right: *Honorable mention All-Mountain West Conference line-backer Tommy Hackenbruck.*

TOM SMART

SCOTT G. WINTERTON

Bottom Left: *Safety Eric Weddle was named second team All-Mountain West Conference.*

Bottom Right: *Punter Matt Kovacevich punted his way to an honorable mention selection on the All-Mountain West Conference team.*

TOM SMART

Left: Kyle Whittingham addresses the media after accepting the head coaching job at Utah. He spent 11 years as an assistant with the Utes before being picked to replace Urban Meyer, who accepted the head coaching job at Florida after two seasons in Salt Lake City.

Right: Jamie and Kyle Whittingham listen as Utah athletic director Chris Hill announces that the former BYU star is the new leader of the Utes.

UTAH UTES

A UTAH MAN!
Whittingham Press Conference

TOM SMART

Kyle Whittingham To Take The Reins of the Utah Program

As far as telephone conversations go, the late night conversation between Kyle Whittingham and Utah athletic director Chris Hill wasn't all that intriguing. Its content, however, proved to be quite significant.

"I'm in," Whittingham told Hill. "I can't deal with it anymore. Let's move forward."

And just like that, the Utes had hired a new head football coach – one to replace Urban Meyer, who accepted an offer from Florida.

"When he called me I could tell by his voice that he really wanted to get this thing going," said Hill, who signed

TOM SMART

Bottom Left: *Kyle Whittingham gives his mother a hug at the press conference where he was named Utah's new head coach.*

Top Right: *Utah quarterback Alex Smith meets with reporters in the new indoor practice facility. He was happy that a member of Urban Meyer's staff was hired as head coach.*

Bottom Right: *After weighing an offer to coach at his alma mater BYU, Kyle Whittingham opted to become Utah's head coach instead.*

TOM SMART

TOM SMART

TOM SMART

Whittingham to a six-year contract worth $675,000 annually.

The agreement ended five days of consternation and speculation as Whittingham also mulled over an offer to coach his alma mater BYU. The former Cougar linebacker and graduate assistant said he lost 11 pounds while getting just 11 hours worth of sleep during the process.

"It was a difficult decision and that's no secret," said Whittingham. "It took time."

One that ultimately came down, as it turned out, to already being where he wanted to be.

"It's a great opportunity. One that I've had my eye on for 11 years now," Whittingham said at a press conference December 8, 2004 at Rice-Eccles Stadium. "I'm just thrilled to be in this position."

Whittingham apologized to BYU and athletic administrator Tom Holmoe, who he insists did everything right, for having his decision-making process turn into a "dog and pony show." The new Ute coach said he has a lot of respect for the school where he played football and earned two degrees and wanted to make that clear.

"The pendulum just kept swinging back and forth. These were two great opportunities," said Whittingham, who ultimately resolved the issue with logic. "When in doubt don't. I feel comfortable here."

Whittingham is completing his 11th season on the Utah staff, including the past 10 as defensive coordinator. He takes control of a fifth-ranked program that has won 15 straight games over two years and is headed to the Fiesta Bowl on January 1, 2005 to face Pittsburgh.

"It is with great delight that we were able to persuade him that this was the right opportunity," said university president Michael K. Young. "Because it's certainly right for the University of Utah."

Hill denied reports out of Las Vegas that former Utah offensive coordinator Mike Sanford, who is now the head coach at UNLV, was the top choice to fill the vacancy.

Whittingham was quickly identified as the top candidate in a quick process that began with Meyer's resignation December 3 at noon. Approximately three hours later, Hill and Whittingham met to discuss the opening.

Soon after, Hill told his wife Kathy that the search was over.

"This is our guy," he revealed to her. "We've got to figure out how to get him."

Players and donors, alike, applaud the hiring.

"We're going to play our hearts out for this guy," said sophomore safety Eric Weddle. "It's huge to have him here at Utah. It's going to be awesome just to keep this thing going."

After days of speculation, senior captain Morgan Scalley said the Utes can now breathe a sigh of relief. They got their man.

"He commands respect," said Scalley. "He does not put up with a lot of flack,If you're not doing what's right on and off the field, you're not going to be part of this program."

Whittingham's unwavering commitment to his players, his stable influence and positive attitude, along with an ability to meet challenges, are some of the traits that caught Hill's attention.

Spence Eccles, whose financial contributions to the program have been well documented, acknowledged that he and other big donors are pleased with decision to hire Whittingham.

"I would say that we made it abundantly clear what we felt was the best long-term direction for the program and who was the best guy at this time," said Eccles. "It's the right time for the right man at the right place."

Whittingham announced that former Southern Utah coach Gary Andersen would replace him as defensive coordinator . Less than a week later, Oregon assistant Andy Ludwig was named offensive coordinator.

"I'm excited about keeping what we've got going with Urban Meyer. The discipline structure, the academics, everything he put in place I firmly believe in. But, it's not going to be Urban Meyer, part two," said Whittingham, who noted his flavor and personality will be incorporated into schemes. "The direction that we're heading right now is where we're going to stay. Expectations are high."

Meyer was contacted about the hiring in an early morning telephone call from Coach Anderson.

"He's a Utah man, sir," Meyer was told.

"First of all, it's well deserved," said Meyer, who recommended Whittingham for the job. "Utah's officially a top-20 program with this move."

TOM SMART

New Utah head football coach Kyle Whittingham brought a smile to athletic director Chris Hill's face at a Rice-Eccles Stadium press conference to announce his hiring.

UNIVERSITY OF UTAH

Welcome to the Fiesta Bowl

JEFFREY D. ALLRED

JEFFREY D. ALLRED

JEFFREY D. ALLRED

PRE-BOWL FESTIVITIES

Opposite: *Mike McFly (R) and Cory Jackson paint the University of Utah endzone in Sun Devil Stadium in preparation for the Fiesta Bowl.*

Below: *University of Utah football co-coaches Kyle Whittingham and Urban Meyer (L) speak to the media at the airport in Phoenix, Arizona upon their arrival for the Fiesta Bowl.*

JEFFREY D. ALLRED

It didn't take long for defensive tackle Sione Pouha and the rest of the Utes to realize the Fiesta Bowl was something special.

Utah's arrival at Sky Harbor Airport was heralded with a welcoming ceremony on the tarmac. Bowl officials, sporting their familiar yellow jackets, rolled out a red carpet and applauded as Pouha led the procession past a mariachi band and dozens of well-wishers who waved signs of support.

JEFFREY D. ALLRED

Top Left: *University of Utah football co-coaches Kyle Whittingham (R) and Urban Meyer speak to the media with the Fiesta Bowl trophy on display.*

Bottom Left: *University of Utah football team member Sione Pouha shoots some video of the Fiesta Bowl Quenn Lindsey Taylor (r) and her court Jessica Wheeler, Tina Zabalza and Kelsey Massee. They welcomed the Utes December 26, 2004 at the airport in Phoenix, Arizona upon their arrival for the Fiesta Bowl.*

JEFFREY D. ALLRED

JEFFREY D. ALLRED

JEFFREY D. ALLRED

JEFFREY D. ALLRED

Left Top: *University of Utah football player Morgan Scalley has some fun talking with a Fiesta Bowl Youth Gridiron Day participant December 27th, 2004 at Scottsdale Community College in Scottsdale, Arizona. Local youth organizations were invited to interact with coaches and players.*

Left Bottom: *A band plays while welcoming the University of Utah football team at the airport in Phoenix, Arizona upon their arrival for the Fiesta Bowl.*

"I guess that's why they call it the BCS," said Pouha. "Look at it. Everybody is just trying to soak it in."

The welcome, he added, was in sharp contrast to a year ago when a lone Elvis Presley impersonator met the team at the Memphis airport prior to the Liberty Bowl.

"We're excited to be here," said Pouha. "This is the real deal."

Morgan Scalley, who is also a senior captain, acknowledged the greeting was special.

"I've never had someone so excited to have me be anywhere - including my wife," he joked. "It's good to be here. They're very hospitable. We're excited and ready to get things rolling."

After a short press conference featuring coaches Urban Meyer and Kyle Whittingham, the Utes checked into the ritzy Scottsdale Plaza Hotel. They later practiced at nearby Scottsdale Community College.

"I think they're in awe and they should be," said Meyer. "They also prepare very well."

It's that balance, added quarterback Alex Smith, that the fifth-ranked Utes hope to achieve in seeking their 12th win and making history as the first team from a conference without an automatic berth to crash the financially lucrative Bowl Championship Series.

"This is what this team has worked so hard to get," said Smith. "It would be a shame if we didn't enjoy this."

It's a dream come true, noted Meyer.

"We are so proud to be here. This is a once-in-a-lifetime opportunity," he said. "I told our players, 'You'll go to other bowl games, but they'll be nothing like the Fiesta Bowl.'"

During their week in Arizona, the Utes squeezed appearances and other social events into an already busy schedule that included daily practices and team meetings.

Before leaving the practice facility Monday, they interacted with several Phoenix-area youth organizations as part of Fiesta Bowl Youth Gridiron Day.

On Thursday, Utah's players and coaches attended at 45-minute pep rally at a resort near South Mountain, where the alumni association had set up headquarters. Several thousand fans attended the gathering that featured remarks

Right: *Utah fans enjoy the New Year's Eve Tostitos Fiesta Bowl Block Party in downtown Tempe.*

MITCH DUMKE

JEFFREY D. ALLRED

TOM SMART

Top Left: *Thousands of Ute fans were on hand to cheer on the University of Utah football team at a pep rally in Phoenix, Arizona.*

Bottom Left: *Sione Pouha leads the crowd as fans and players enjoy a pep rally.*

by team captains Morgan Scalley, Bo Nagahi, Paris Warren, Alex Smith and Pouha. Meyer and defensive coordinator Kyle Whittingham also spoke to the appreciative crowd. The cheerleaders, Crimson Line and the Ute Marching Band were also on hand.

The University of Utah staged the event as a gift to the Crimson Club, the MUSS and other Ute fans for their season-long support. The Fiesta Bowl parade, a New Year's Eve Block Party and game-day tailgating party followed as the much-anticipated game finally arrived.

Below: *University of Utah football team members, led by Morgan Scalley, talk at a pep rally December 30th, 2004 in Phoenix, Arizona. Thousands of Ute fans were on hand.*

JEFFREY D. ALLRED

PAGE 125

Top Left: *The University of Utah band participates in the Fort McDowell Fiesta Bowl parade December 31st, 2004 in Phoenix, Arizona.*

Bottom Left: *Football players are greeted by fans as they arrive at a pep rally.*

Top Right: *Young Utah fans take a photo from their cell phone to document the moment as Utah fans enjoy the New Year's Eve Tostitos Fiesta Bowl Block Party in downtown Tempe.*

Bottom Right: *The University of Utah Crimson Line led by Megan Terry participate in the Fort McDowell Fiesta Bowl parade.*

JEFFREY D. ALLRED

TOM SMART

TOM SMART

JEFFREY D. ALLRED

TOM SMART

Swoop jokes with the crowd as fans and players enjoy a pep rally on Thursday night, December 30, 2004.

TOM SMART

***Above:** Utah fans enjoy the New Year's Eve Tostitos Fiesta Bowl Block Party in downtown Tempe.*

***Right:** Thousands of Utah fans enjoy the New Year's Eve Tostitos Fiesta Bowl Block Party.*

MITCH DUMKE

ParkiT

TOSTITOS
FIESTA BOWL
26:17

Opposite: The Utah marching band performs prior to the start of the Fiesta Bowl in Tempe, AZ, January 1, 2005.

Right: The University of Utah's co-head coach Urban Meyer shouts on the sidelines during the second half of the Fiesta Bowl.

FIESTA BOWL: Utah 35, Pittsburg 7

Saturday, January 1, 2005: Tempe, Arizona

JEFFREY D. ALLRED

Utah's quest for perfection is complete.

Undefeated, Unchallenged: Storybook season ends with big victory

A 35-7 win over Pittsburgh in the Tostitos Fiesta Bowl capped a 12-0 season for the Utes, who made quite a splash in their Bowl Championship Series debut.

"In today's day and age of college football going undefeated is hard to do. There's a lot of great teams out there," said head coach Urban Meyer, who finished his two-year stint at Utah with a 22-2 record. "It's hard to say goodbye, but I'm saying goodbye 12-0. What a great effort by our guys. This is the best group I've ever been around."

Utah quarterback Alex Smith and wide receiver Paris Warren were named co-Offensive Players of the Game and nose guard Steve Fifita claimed defensive honors.

JEFFREY D. ALLRED

Top Right: *The University of Utah's Steve Fifita sacks Pitt QB Tyler Palko during the second half action.*

Bottom Right: *Fans celebrate a perfect season by the Utes.*

Below: *Fireworks fly over Sun Devil Stadium before the 2005 Fiesta Bowl in Tempe, AZ.*

MITCH DUMKE

TOM SMART

MITCH DUMKE

"It wasn't an easy game," said Warren. "We just executed well in all three phases."

The offense shined with 467 yards and 25 first downs. Smith completed 29-of-37 passes for 328 yards and four touchdowns. Warren scored twice and caught a Fiesta Bowl-record 15 catches.

TOM SMART

Defensively, the Utes racked up nine sacks while limiting the Panthers to just 268 yards. Eric Weddle led the way with a game-high 11 tackles and Tommy Hackenbruck had three sacks.

"We blitzed them a lot. We gave them a lot of different looks," said Fifita. "I don't know how to explain the pressure we got. We just saw openings and took advantage of them."

Besides a convincing performance on the field, they also did well in the stands. A vast majority of the sellout crowd of 73,519 at Sun Devil Stadium wore red in support of the BCS busters. Utah is the first team from a conference without an automatic bid to participate in one of the system's financially lucrative bowl games. The expected payout is between $14-17 million.

Smith said the victory sent a message to the establishment.

"Hopefully that college football needs a few changes," he said. "That's been the mind set all along."

Utah received the Fiesta Bowl championship trophy in a postgame ceremony on the field. Amidst the celebration, the large contingent of Ute fans chanted "undefeated" to the team and "one more year" to Smith, who is contemplating a jump to the NFL and its riches.

The Utes cashed in early and often against the Panthers. They built a 28-0 lead midway through the third quarter while cruising to their school record-tying 16th consecutive victory. The streak equals a mark established in 1930, the last time a Utah team went unbeaten or untied.

Warren scored twice down the stretch to give the Utes a pair of 28-point leads. Less than six minutes after hauling in a 23-yard touchdown pass from Smith, Warren took a hook-and-ladder

Center: *Marty Johnson runs for a touchdown during third quarter action in the Fiesta Bowl.*

Right: *The University of Utah's Paris Warren leaps over a teammate on the way to his first touchdown of the night.*

JEFFREY D. ALLRED

pass from teammate Steve Savoy for another score.

Between touchdowns, Pitt scored its first points of the game on a 31-yard pass from Tyler Palko to Greg Lee.

The Panthers (8-4), however, were never in contention after a sluggish start. Their problems were compounded by Marty Johnson's 18-yard touchdown run on the Utes' first series in the second half.

Utah continued a season-long streak of leading at halftime by holding a 14-0 advantage. The Utes scored touchdowns on two of their first three possessions to pull away from the Panthers. The first score

JEFFREY D. ALLRED

JEFFREY D. ALLRED

RECAP
FIESTA BOWL

Pittsburgh	0	0	7	0	- 7
Utah	7	7	21	0	- 35

UTAH - Ganther, Quinton 4 yd run (Carroll, David kick), 03:09, 1st

UTAH - Madsen, John 6 yd pass from Smith, Alex (Carroll kick) 05:29, 2nd

UTAH - Johnson, Marty 18 yd pass from Smith, Alex (Carroll kick) 11:13, 3rd

UTAH - Warren, Paris 23 yd pass from Smith, Alex (Carroll kick) 06:22, 3rd

PITT - Lee,Greg 31 yd pass from Palko, Tyler (Cummings, Josh kick) 04:28, 3rd

UTAH -Warren, Paris 18 yd pass from Smith, Alex (Carroll kick) 00:25, 3rd

PITT	FINAL STATISTICS	UTAH
19	First Downs	25
30-17	Net Rushing	31-139
251	Passing Yards	328
268	Total Offense	467
31:17	Time of Possession	28:43

Top Left: *Utah's Marquess Ledbetter celebrates with Reza Williams after a sack of the Pitt QB during the first half of the Fiesta Bowl.*

Bottom Left: *The Utes celebrate their victory in the 2005 Fiesta Bowl.*

PAGE 134
Top Left: *Young fans cheer on the Utes during their win in the Fiesta Bowl.*

Bottom Left: *Spencer Toone tackles Pitt quarterback Tyler Palko.*

Top Right: *Sione Pouha (90) and Steve Fifita celebrate one of the four sacks that Utah recorded in the first two quarters.*

Bottom Right: *A University of Utah fan shows his true colors before the start of the Fiesta Bowl.*

TOM SMART

TOM SMART

TOM SMART

TOM SMART

came late in the first quarter when Quinton Ganther reached the end zone on a 4-yard touchdown run. The second came on a 6-yard scoring strike from Smith to John Madsen with 5:29 remaining in the half.

Defense and special teams also made contributions. The Utes recorded four quarterback sacks over the first and second quarters while holding Pitt scoreless. The Panthers attempted a 48-yard field goal between Utah touchdowns, but it was blocked by freshman Martail Burnett.

"We obviously ran into an excellent football team. I think in the physical parts of the game we did not match up," said Pittsburgh coach Walt Harris. "We had trouble on offense protecting our passer. On defense, you know, I think they put the pressure on people all year long and that's why they score big."

The fifth-ranked Utes have now won four consecutive bowl games. The streak includes the Las Vegas Bowl in 1999 and 2001 as well as the 2003 Liberty Bowl. The last two victories came under Meyer, who officially turned over control of the program to long-time defensive coordinator Kyle Whittingham.

MITCH DUMKE

The University of Utah's Alex Smith runs for yardage in the first half of the Fiesta Bowl.

JEFFREY D. ALLRED

Morgan Scalley leads the charge as Marcus Furman is brought down during the first half.

TOM SMART

The University of Utah's Quinton Ganther runs for the first touchdown during the first quarter of the 2005 Fiesta Bowl.

TOM SMART

TOM SMART

TOM SMART

TOM SMART

Top Left: *The University of Utah's Ryan Smith plays close defense breaking up a pass to Pitt's Andre Broussard.* ***Top Right:*** *The University of Utah's Morgan Scalley, left, and Steve Fifita bring down Pitt's Tim Murphy during the first quarter action.* ***Bottom Left:*** *The University of Utah's Steve Savoy makes the catch against Pitt's Darrelle Revis.* ***Bottom Right:*** *The University of Utah's John Madsen is congratulated by teammate Travis LaTendresse after Madsen scored the second touchdown for the Utes.*

JEFFREY D. ALLRED

JEFFREY D. ALLRED

JEFFREY D. ALLRED

Left: *Casey Evans celebrates a defensive stop against Pitt during the first half of the Fiesta Bowl.*

Center: *Utah's Eric Weddle looks down on Pitt quarterback Tyler Palko during first half action.*

Right: *Utah's Eric Weddle knocks away a pass intended for Pittsburg's Greg Lee.*

"It's a fairy-tale season and I'm just excited to move forward and continue this program heading in the direction that it's at," said Whittingham.

Opposite: *The American Flag flies at the start of the 2005 Fiesta Bowl in Tempe, AZ, January 1, 2005.*

JEFFREY D. ALLRED

TOM SMART

TOM SMART

Top: *Russ Allred, and his date Marilyn, which he takes to most all of the Utah games, at the tailgate party before the start of the 2005 Fiesta Bowl in Tempe, AZ, January 1, 2005.*

Bottom: *University of Utah fans arrived in Tempe in all shapes, colors and sizes.*

Opposite: *The University of Utah cheerleaders fire up the crowd prior to the start of the Fiesta Bowl.*

TOM SMART

Utah
Style

TOM SMART

Head coach Urban Meyer hugs quarterback Alex Smith as they celebrate their 35-7 victory over Pitt.

TOM SMART

Utah defensive back Ryan Smith holds up a reminder of the Utes undefeated season.

MITCH DUMKE

Coach Urban Meyer takes a moment to reflect on the Utes perfect season.

JEFFREY D. ALLRED

Morgan Scalley, Sione Pouha and Alex Smith celebrate their victory in the 2005 Fiesta Bowl.

TOM SMART

The Utes' Alex Smith is all smiles after their 35-7 victory over Pitt in the 2005 Fiesta Bowl.

JEFFREY D. ALLRED

Sione Pouha dunks Coach Urban Meyer after winning the 2005 Fiesta Bowl.

"This is the best group of young men I've ever been around... It's going to be hard to say goodbye, but we're saying goodbye 12-0."

-Coach Urban Meyer

Opposite: *Outgoing coach Urban Meyer gives the new coach, Kyle Whittingham a hug on the awards stage as Utah wins the Fiesta Bowl by beating Pitt 35-7 January 1, 2005 in Tempe, Arizona.*

TOM SMART

CHAMPIONS

MITCH DUMKE

A special thanks to the following for
their continued support of the University of Utah Football program.

HOT TICKET 700

Marriott
SALT LAKE CITY
UNIVERSITY PARK

OKLAND
CONSTRUCTION